The Complete
Bait Angler's Guide

The Complete Bait Angler's Guide

by Lou Witman

ICS BOOKS, INC.
MERRILLVILLE, INDIANA

THE COMPLETE BAIT ANGLER'S GUIDE

Printed in U.S.A.

Published by:
ICS Books, Inc.
1000 E. 80th Place
Merrillville, IN 46410

Distributed by:
Stackpole Books
Cameron & Kelker
Harrisburg, PA 17105

Library of Congress Cataloging-in-Publication Data

Witman, Lou.
    The complete bait angler's guide.

    Includes index.
    1. Bait. 2. Bait fishing. I. Title.
SH448.W54   1986   799.1'2   86-20834
ISBN 0-934802-32-7

Contents

Chapter 1

Everybody's Bait: The Nightcrawler

They are nose hooked, hooked through the middle, strung on spinners, and globbed on treble hooks. They are trolled, cast, dunked, flipped, and relished by walleyes and carp alike. Big bluegills and bass simply love them, and even the mighty muskellunge has been known to take a swipe at one on occasion. No other live bait is grown, caught, sold or fished as much as *Lubricus terrestries*; the nightcrawler.

Crawlers, as they most often are fondly referred to by angler types, are creatures of the night. These over sized earthworms thrive in clay based soil habitat which allows for their continuous tunneling activities, sometimes reaching a depth of six feet in areas where heavy ground frost has been known to occur. On those nights with the common ingredients of no more than a twenty degree day and night temperature difference, heavy dew or rain; they come to the surface in order to dine on bits of grass, dead leaves, and other delectables.

Figure 1. Farmland, with pasture and the edges of woodlands are prime worm territory for the live baiter.

Top notch nightcrawler territory is worth its weight in gold, especially at today's bait prices, which sees the "dew worm" reach as high as $3.00 per dozen at times in areas of scarcity during July and August. These parcels of priceless real estate can harbor as many as 3,000,000 worms per acre if they are in prime condition. Pastureland that is heavily grazed or mowed for alfalfa is the best choice for the serious worm picker, provided it is not heavily treated with herbicides. Next on the list would be untreated lawns, golf courses, schoolyards, and football fields; and the word untreated entails non-fed or non-fertilized in these urban settings. Strictly natural habitat.

Some years back, golf courses were a heaven for capturing nightcrawlers by the thousands. Much better than pastureland because the grass was mowed two and three times a week, providing a huge food supply for the adult and young worms alike. The short grass also made for quick, easy picking. However, in an effort to make the courses prettier and eliminate most of the weed growth, which has a nasty habit of gathering in stray golf balls thus raising scores and lowering egos, they were chemically treated. This kills most of the worms, and drives the survivors away. A "virgin" golf course is a rare find today, and one closely guarded when one does exist.

Outfitting one's self for the actual capture or harvesting of nightcrawlers is inexpensive, and actually can be done by degrees. If the angler happens to be a one day a week or weekend only fisherman, a couple of dozen worms is usually more than enough for his need. These can be picked out of a small area in the backyard after a thorough soaking with the garden hose when natural precipitation is lacking. One can also opt for the use of either one of the wash into the soil type chemical preparations on the market today or a cattle type prod that injects electrical current into the ground to drive worms to the surface. Both devices are workable for quick harvesting, but they also severely injure the worms you intend to fish with. Needless to say, worms gathered under both methods fall into the "use them quick or lose them" category.

For the more natural, and therefore prolonged longevity and use, method of nightcrawler harvesting, all that is needed is a flashlight, bucket, and a pair of sneakers or soft soled shoes to lessen the vibrations as one moves about. For the nightcrawler fisherman who is lucky enough to be angling two or three days a week, a little more equipment and preparation needs to be done. These anglers may go through a couple of hundred worms a week at times, assuming of course that the fish are biting everywhere but in a mud puddle. Unless they prefer to spend every night out in the backyard picking worms for the next day's outing, they must do things a bit differently. In their case, all the picking can be done in one session for upwards of a couple of weeks' fishing time.

First off, one can not simply walk around the yard bending over like the weekender who needs only a few worms, unless you prefer to have the wife arise the following morning in time to set your coffee cup on the floor and hand you a straw. The best other alternative to keeping the Absorbine Jr. bill below national debt levels is to drop to all fours to do the harvesting. Besides being very quiet, and lessening vibrations to a minimum, the approach is highly efficient and speeds up the worm picking process by allowing the picker to use both hands. This is easily accomplished with the aid of a pair of hip boots or old waders to keep the dampness out of joints, a headlamp and battery, small pouch of sawdust, and a coffee can or bucket.

Headlamps can be found in just about any sporting good store or mail order catalog these days, as they are very popular with frog giggers, and night bowfishermen, along with coon hunters. They are made up of a small lens and bulb attached to an adjustable head band. Also, they usually have around three feet of wire that hooks up to a six volt battery, which slips into an accompanying battery pouch that fits onto a worm picker's belt.

Experienced worm pickers always dim the brightness from either their flashlight or headlamp because of the nightcrawler's extreme sensitivity to light. This can be done effectively by several means. One way is to paint the lens with a light coat of red or yellow enamel. Another method that works as well, and allows the light to be used for other things such as night hunting, is to tape toilet paper or colored tissue paper over the lens. In the absence of tape, rubber bands can be substituted. The only problems with these paper products is that on rainy nights, those best for crawler picking, the paper can get soaked and often falls apart just when you are grabbing like a cotton picker on piece rate.

The small bag of sawdust serves a unique purpose. Under those best conditions, which means wet grass, the nightcrawler picker's hands can not help but get wet. Add to this, the very nature of the nightcrawler's outside skin lubricant which enables him to move underground — slicker than well wetted liver — and you end up with oodles of missed or injured worms. This is especially a problem in harvesting worms early in the year after they have spent a long winter without a lot of food and inactivity that makes them soft, or out of shape if you will. By dipping the fingers or hand into the sawdust every so often, the harvester will not be affected by either the worm's lubricant or the wet conditions quite as much. Ideally, the best way to carry the wood powder is in an old nail pouch that ties around the waist. This keeps it handy, but still out of the way.

The actual picking of nightcrawlers, that is getting them from hole to bucket, is somewhat of an art in itself. More crawlers kick the proverbial bucket from bruising, stretching, and other rough handling than from anything else, save rotten care, and this does not show up immediately. They can die within hours, a few days, or even a week.

Crawlers seldom come out of their burrows completely, unless they are forced to do so from below by another worm, or perhaps the threat of drowning because of burrow flooding. Instead, they extend themselves about two thirds of the way out to feed, and when danger threatens, quickly retreat with the aid of their powerful tails. This tail — they can move up to 60 times their own weight with its amazing strength — is the main problem for the worm harvester.

When a crawler is grabbed, he immediately anchors his tail by spreading it to keep from being pulled from the hole. If you have ever watched a bird work on getting a worm dinner you know it's so. That is what gives birds hernias, and why they have tail feathers to keep from falling head over heels if the worm breaks, which it often does. The key for us humans capturing nightcrawlers is to make the grab as close to the burrow opening as possible, and quickly pull him out before he has a chance to anchor. Failing that, the only thing to do is keep up a steady pressure until he weakens or relaxes to try and get a better grip with his tail. A worm can then be slipped quickly out of the burrow.

Naturally, there are going to be times when a worm is grabbed close to his head, near the breeding ring, or somewhere else besides the preferred target area. In such circumstances, aged worm pickers use a couple of neat tricks to "get their worm", as they say, without damage.

Crawlers have a peculiar habit in that which ever end is touched, they move in the opposite direction, even though the opposite end can not go anywhere. If a nightcrawler is pinned by the head or near it, and does have a chance to anchor its tail, many times its rear can be coaxed right out by simply touching it lightly with a finger.

Another gimmick to get tough worms from their homes to the bucket is to suddenly release them after the picker has applied a long steady pull. The crawler will relax just long enough, in order to recoil back into the burrow. If he is grabbed as soon as this movement is observed, the worm will easily come out of his sanctuary.

Once one has captured enough worms for his or her fishing, then comes the real task, which is keeping nightcrawlers alive and in the best condition possible for their day on the lake, river, or stream. A fat, healthy crawler will go a lot farther towards providing a full stringer at day's end than will one that is limp, skinny, and practically lifeless.

Of critical importance in keeping your nightcrawlers healthy and happy is the bedding. Never keep crawlers in plain soil, manure, leaves, grass, or wood chips. Yes, that is correct. I did say, "wood chips". Believe it or not, there are those who advise others to do so.

I had occasion, in the not too distant past, to venture into a bait shop where the owner was rather new at the live bait game. Next to his counter sat three very large bags of wood chips. I asked what they were for. His response was to reach into his bait refrigerator and pull out one of the standard styrofoam boxes, called flats, that nightcrawlers are stored in full of — you guessed it — wood chips and worms. Quizzing him on where he had come up with the idea, I learned somebody had come in that morning and sold him both the nightcrawlers and wood bedding. Of course, they were running a special. I quickly explained that wood was not particularly suited for any type of earthworm. Termites yes, but nightcrawlers? Definitely not! Like a chicken who wants to chew bubblegum, crawlers lack an appreciable denture capability, thus doing about as well at ingesting wood as the bird does blowing bubbles. Besides that, wood can't hold any amount of water, which is critical.

Probably the most common misconception about what to store crawlers in is that plain old earth or dirt if you like, is good. Many believe that soil would be great naturally since it is the medium that the worms live in. Not so. Crawlers live in burrows in solidly packed earth. Loose soil coats their exterior by clinging to their slimy skin, thus clogging pores and smothering them in much the same way a human would smother if their body was coated with paint.

Loose grass, leaves and manure are not for keeping crawlers either. All three have the property of giving off heat and gases as they decompose, which can be deadly to the worms. Rather, the ideal material for keeping nightcrawlers in is one of the commercial paper pulp beddings, such as Buss Bedding, specifically made for this purpose. With this substance, crawlers can be kept almost indefinitely with the proper maintenance. In fact, the crawlers will sometimes even breed and lay eggs in the material as if in their own environment.

This paper mulch, as one might call it, comes in a dry cotton like state, and must have water added. It should be thoroughly mixed by hand, and the proper consistency is achieved when the bedding is moist, but not wet. The best judgement can be made by squeezing a handful firmly after mixing. If more than a few drops of water are wrung out, the bedding is too wet, and more will have to be mixed in to dry it out a little.

Perhaps the worst enemy of all where the safe keeping of nightcrawlers is concerned is temperature. Direct sun, and its ultraviolet rays is definitely out, whether in a boat while fishing, or just storing crawlers. The direct rays will kill crawlers in minutes, and covered containers will heat up and kill them in an hour or so at most. Ideal temperature for storing crawlers falls between 40 and 60 degrees, with maximum benefits coming at the mid to lower ends of this range.

When storing nightcrawlers for an extended period, the bedding should be checked for moisture loss, and diseased or injured worms. The moisture loss can be retarded a great deal by placing several layers of wet newspaper on top of the bedding itself. Any "bad" worms should be removed at once. These can be identified easily by limpness, swollen areas, and discolored spots in the body.

The right container goes a long way towards the proper care of crawlers too. Years back, when one could get licorice for a penny or thereabouts, early crawler flats that bait dealers used were made of wood. With the advent of styrofoam, these were quickly discarded. Styrofoam has the qualities of breathing much like the soil nightcrawlers live in, and at the same time, it also insulates against heat. Any styrofoam cooler will do a good job in storing crawlers, as long as it is not over-crowded. However, the very best are the ones used by tropical fish dealers to ship their goods. One used to be able to get these free from local pet shops, but when demand became great, the bright light of the dollar sign came on. Worm keepers will now have to pay a price for them. I must say though, that the price is worth paying when considering how much in bait losses they can save.

In situations where nightcrawlers are being kept for long periods, the bedding will have to be changed completely on occasion. The crawlers will be eating some of it, and gradually their wastes and body juices will render it harmful to them. The material will have the look of small, dry grayish pebbles when it reaches this state, and will lack any solidity or consistency as it did when first mixed.

After a batch of crawlers is captured and ready to place in their new home, it should be done in the following manner. Some crawlers are bound to be bruised or otherwise injured. This is inevitable to some degree. When placing the worms in the bait box, they should simply be put on top of the bedding. Healthy crawlers will work their way into the bedding without any trouble. Injured and dying worms will remain on top, and these should be discarded within twelve hours or so.

In the early spring or mid-fall months, maintaining the ideal temperatures outdoors is no problem as long as the container is in a shaded area. During the summer months, other preparations must be made.

An old, but working refrigerator is an ideal worm container once the shelves are removed. As many as four or five flats can be stacked inside once this is accomplished. Garage sales, swap shops, and appliance stores are likely places to pick one up for a reasonable price. There is one tip that applies to keeping worms in a refer, and that is to either keep them covered or fix it so the interior light remains on. Since nightcrawlers are nocturnal by nature, you might otherwise open the door to find a full fledged wormherd stampede on your hand, floor, etc.

One other inexpensive means to store nightcrawlers is to place them underground. All that really need be done in this case is to dig a square pit around 30"x30" and at least three feet deep in a shaded area. The bottom should be lined with at least a couple of inches of fine gravel to allow for any water to run off, and keep the worms in. A cover made from two by fours and plywood with either shingles, aluminum, or a couple of coats of white paint to deflect the sun and keep the interior cool, will finish the job.

Utilizing the same type of cover, an old bath tub will do well as a worm holder also when buried underground. With one, you won't need the gravel lining, since the built in drain will serve the same purpose. However, don't fail to put a piece of galvanized fine wire screen over it to prevent an industrious worm from gaining freedom, or a like endowed mole from getting in. Virtually all of these means will allow the nightcrawler catcher to store all the worms he needs for just about any fishing endeavor he chooses.

Chapter 2

Cousins to the Crawler:
Leaf & Redworms

If nightcrawlers get the votes as the most used live baits, some of their smaller cousins cannot be too far behind. A true statement especially where fisherfolk prefer to angle for the likes of bluegills, perch, rock bass, and other members of the panfish clan; as well as many a small stream trouter who swear by these smaller versions as well.

Belonging to the 3000 member *Oligochaeta* class of the *Annelid* or segmented worm family, cousins they truly are, and with lots of aunts and uncles too. Like their larger relative, both leaf and redworms function in the same manner, spending their lives breeding and digesting organic material. In the case of the leafworm, who is in reality a small or immature nightcrawler in many localities, and a true worm in its own right in others, their name gives a clue to primary habitat.

Deciduous trees, those that shed their leaves at seasonal interludes, provide them with their primary habitat. Areas along roads,

10

fields with some type of wind break or fence line, and city or county landfills are excellent spots for leaf piles to accumulate. The leaves provide all the necessary ingredients for year around growth and comfort, as well as nursery facilities for the earthworms. As they break down, the tree cast offs give warmth in the winter, and at the same time are food all year long. In the summer months, the rainfall they soak up from spring thaws and storms provides the moisture and cooling that is life sustaining. But! Not any old leaf pile does a home for leafworms make, so just the mere act of locating one is no guarantee of a population of fish bait.

Even before leaf looking, the first consideration when exploring a likely area for leafworms is soil type. As will their larger brethren, clay based soils are by far the best with sandy soil the worst. Other points worthy of deliberation, especially when leaf piles themselves are neither large nor extensive, are shade and additional grassy area for added moisture content and food, should the worms need it in times of little rain.

The leaf piles are tops when at least 50% decomposed. New piles have two problems; that of not being broken down enough biologically speaking to provide a really ample food source, and at times too warm and gaseous in the first stages of this process. Also, particular leaf types can make a difference in certain instances.

Although far from any basis of purely scientific and all encompassing study on the part of this fisherman, the better spots seem to be where mixtures of different varieties of leaves such as maple, elm, birch, etc. for example occur. With the exception of the maples, which always seem to harbor leafworms, piles that are dominated by one particular type do not produce nearly as well. This is especially true where oaks are concerned, which have a high tannic acid count that keeps worms at a distance, at least until the piles are almost completely decomposed.

For those harvesters hard pressed to get a batch of worms to go fishing, hunting on short notice, and having to take pot luck where they can obtain it, one can get by. These "not so hot" spots can give up a few worms if a couple of wrinkles are employed. If you have the option of a next morning trip, try hunting the edges of these piles after dark. Many times those worms in the vicinity

will come to the surface along the edges to pick at the leaves and
dead grass there once the light of day is gone. It won't hurt your
chances any to wet down the area at dusk either, especially if it
has been a while since the last rainfall.

The other alternative is to spade up the vicinity if you are
really up against the proverbial wall. Either that or use one of the
chemical products mentioned in the nightcrawler section to force
worms to the surface. Once up and picked, rinse them with some
water to keep damage to a minimum.

Thanks to the fact that the name Leafworm is a bit of a mis-
nomer, leaf piles are not the only habitat that anglers need search
to get at these fish morsels. Bluntly, leafworms can be had far
away from trees if you know where to look, or in plain old dirt in
other words.

Best soil types to actually dig up a bunch of leafworms is of
the rich black variety such as that found along rivers or creeks,
septic systems, barnyards, and low land meadows. You can also
hunt them in the same manner as crawlers, that is with a light —
on your knees — if you are not inclined to make like a coal miner.

Tools of the trade for do-it-yourself leafworming should
include a small hand rake, spade for occasional dirt digging, metal-
styrofoam-or plastic bucket, and a pair of cheap cotton gloves. The
gloves will serve to keep hands from getting cut or scratched in
the inevitable glass and other human debris common to a lot of leaf
piles in our modern "use and pitch it" world.

Leafworm storage basically follows along the same lines as
that of crawler storage. The only difference is that the leafworms
can be stored in the same material they were gathered from. Also,
a little black dirt should be added to this natural bedding to keep
up the moisture content, especially if the leaves are not quite
thoroughly broken down. Most of the time however, the leaf piles
that contain the largest batches of worms will be in fine enough
shape so that all one has to do is place it in a styrofoam container
for storage.

Before moving on, there is one thing that a leafworm harvester
must be careful of when using natural bedding, and that is to make
sure the material is completely free from ants. These little devils

will devour any worm they come across. I learned this lesson the hard way some years back when I pulled three flats from my refrigerator, only to find them full of still hungry little ants, and not one single leafworm.

Getting and keeping on hand enough leafworms to satisfy the needs of more than a day or so of fishing can obviously be a problem for some anglers, especially if viable hunting spots are rare. For those not inclined to find the time and keep up a prolonged effort, the solution comes in by way of your own worm development.

Basically, worm developments are not much different, with the exception that the inhabitants have no legs as compared to two legs, than a housing development used by us humans. Someone comes in and builds a group of dwellings, and soon thereafter, the living quarters are filled with either people or worms. With a worm development however, one has two advantages. No nosey neighbors and a fair amount of bonus nightcrawlers as well.

In order to get the maximum number of leafworms to occupy your efforts, site location is all important. Best areas are those heavily shaded so that both leaves and ground will hold plenty of moisture, just as those prime spots in the wild do. The area used does not in itself have to be a large one. Twenty foot by twenty foot is plenty.

Once a sight is chosen, the next step is to place a sturdy post that is around thirty-six inches long in each corner of the site. An eight inch ditch or trench is then dug, connecting each post. Galvanized wire, with a mesh measurement of a half inch or less is placed in the trench, and the upper part is stapled to the posts. This is done to keep out moles, which will quickly clean out the now easy pickin' worms if they get into your worm beds. Also, the wire helps to alleviate white hair and heart attack, along with premature ageing. That is what most worm gatherers quickly acquire while busily harvesting and make the wholly unintentional mistake of grabbing a snake who has chosen to rest in the cool darkness of a leaf pile.

After the galvanized wire is covered with the soil from the trenching, the only thing left to do for the new worm farmer is to gather enough leaves to make a blanket of tree leavings about 12-18 inches deep. In order to keep the leaves damp, and speed up the breakdown process a little, use the garden hose to wet them down each day for about a week. Within a few weeks, depending on the time of year, worms should start moving in steadily, and within a couple of months, be providing anglers with enough fishing bait. As the leaves compact, the only added maintenance is to add a few more leaves every so often.

Redworms

A great many bluegill anglers simply hate the thought of going out into the lake without a cup or two of redworms, and truly dedicated red-ear sunfishermen simply do not go fishing unless redworms are along. Reds, as they are often labeled, are actually a manure worm for the most part. Usually smaller in diameter than leafworms, they are also distinctly different in appearance with a brownish-red hue, and have tiny yellow rings around the entire body. Although unrealized by the majority of fishermen, it's these little yellow rings that have a great deal to do with their fish appeal. This stems from the fact that they are a dead ringer for a worm called *Tubifex tubifex*, which is an aquatic realtive that lives in soft bottoms of rivers, lakes, and streams where many fish spend a lot of time grubbing or rooting for them.

Although not likely to make your hands render the aroma of a bunch of roses, redworms are perhaps the easiest of all worms to gather, keep, and-or raise. All one needs in the way of tools is a bucket, pronged digger or pitch fork, and a barnyard with an ample supply of manure supplied by a few horses, cattle, or hogs. Like their other relatives, leafworms and crawlers, reds live off the organic material — undigested bits of grain, grass, etc. — found in the wastes of these farm animals in this case. The manure is just the medium in which it happens to be located, and additionally provides a home for the worms.

Raising redworms is as easy as gathering them, once a batch of manure is gathered. It can be placed in many types of containers such as wash tubs, old bath tubs, or watering troughs or tanks. As with leaf piles, manure should be aged a bit before adding worms. Better yet is to collect some with worms already on the premises.

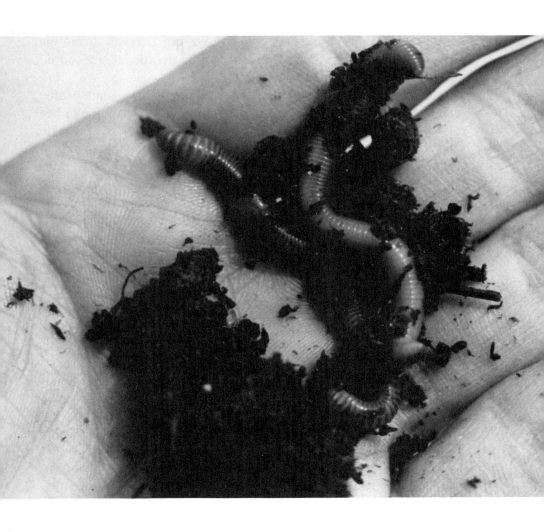

Figure 2. Redworms, distinguished by those little yellow bands, resemble an aquatic relative, hence their effectiveness.

That way, all one has to do is pick the adults for use, letting the juveniles grow up and produce additional worms.

Old timers generally prefer horse manure over that of cattle or hogs. The equine leavings break down quicker and do not get quite as warm, so if you need to add worms in order to get started, the process is quickened somewhat.

It is a good idea to place the containers in a shaded area, although this is more of a moisture retaining factor than one of heat retardation because reds withstand a warmer environment far better than either of their worm family relatives. Either tanks, tubs, or troughs should be drilled to allow for adequate drainage of some sort to prevent water gathering in the bottoms.

If one prefers, manure can just be piled on the ground instead of placed in holding containers. This is without a doubt, the least expensive and complicated approach. The piles should be at least three feet in height, and around four feet wide to provide the reds with plenty of room and depth to get away from dryness in no rain times.

In all cases, whether tubs or ground piles are in use, keep in mind that the redworm will simply up and move out should things break down to the point that the manure no longer provides the necessities. When the natural bedding gets to the point that it is dry and the consistency of a sawdust like state, it's time for new material. What you do with the old is to put it to use in the flower beds or garden. That can be a plus, especially if your better half is not a fisherman who understands the needs of having a prime, juicy worm on hand when you get the urge for fish filets.

Chapter 3

Big and Little Fish Baits:
Crabs-Leeches-Sallies & Frogs

In this modern day fishing world of fast bass boats, oxygen meters, graphs, and pH, the patriarch anglers of long ago are most often forgotten. Today's sport was weaned on the use of live bait by these men. The mention of live bait in our time and space generally brings minnows and worms to the minds of most. Granted, these two baits play as major a role in fish taking today as yesterday, but when it came time to seek the over-paunched largemouth in the lilies, or monstrous tooth filled pike cruising the last remnants of cabbage in the autumn, the old sages turned many times to other live wiggling things.

Crayfish

With few exceptions, fish just about any river or stream in the country, and you need not take any bait along. Just flip over a few rocks, and you will have at least enough to catch a fish or two.

Crabs, craws, crawdads, or crayfish as local labels go, the fresh-water lobster look alikes are one of the most available and fish

17

catching baits that modern live bait enthusiasts can put to use. Venturing from underwater burrows, rock crevices and other hide-outs, once waters warm sufficiently in the springtime, crayfish can be found in ponds, lakes, streams and rivers until the following fall when cool waters once again send them to a semi-hibernetic state.

The general habitat of these freshwater crustaceans during the warm water period varies widely, depending upon size as much as what is available to hide out in. The older crayfish, from about three inches up, often like to take up residence under rocks or logs if they are available. Smaller craws do not venture out in search of food like their older cousins and relatives. Instead, they prefer to eat right where they live to avoid exposure to predators, and that entails the previously mentioned relation. Patches of vegetation and waterlogged leaf piles harbor large numbers of the little crabs in their juvenile state, which usually begins when they reach about a half inch long. Prior to this, they will have begun life, once hatched, hanging onto the underbelly of their mother.

Crawdads can be gathered quite easily in either daylight or under the cover of darkness, which is their natural activity period for the most part. However, methods one chooses to employ will govern, more or less, which period is used.

For those inclined towards the excitement of the hunt and chase, plus a little added "danger" in the way of a sharp nip by a claw, hunting crabs by day with bare hands is a good choice. It also has the appeal of being far from complicated. The crawdad prospector wades slowly and quietly from rock to rock — or other hiding place — gently lifting each in turn so as not to spook the quarry. Once spotted, the crab is unceremoniously grabbed, and tossed into a waiting bucket.

Equipment needs are as minimal as the effort in this particular phase of bait gathering. Besides the bucket, which can be held between the knees — attached to a belt — or buoyed with the aid of small innertube, a pair of hip boots or waders will finish the job. Even these are not strictly called for. Given warm enough conditions, many crabbers just use an old pair of sneakers and shorts, wading wet as it were.

Of course, some of us are not as coordinated or mobile as others, meaning clumsy at times, which also translates to a little trouble being quick enough to put the grab on the crab. I do not particularly have an overt fondness for getting nipped by the small — yet strong — claws these crustaceans carry either, hence my remedy for both maladies if conditions let me get away with it.

A common household coffee can of the 3 lb. variety is the ticket for this modified approach. Once the rock or whatever has been moved, the can, which has previously had both ends removed, is dropped over the crab. Unless one has the hands of the Empire State Building Ape, any crab hunter can use a small fish net to reach in and scoop up his intended fish catcher with ease, and transfer him to the waiting bait bucket.

For gathering large numbers of crayfish, as well as the smaller ones so enticing to panfish in a hurry, the do-it-yourself bait getter can select to make use of a seine.

Perhaps the most common description of a seine is that they are nothing more than elongated fish nets, running from around six foot to very large versions most likely used by a canning company for fish harvesting. Their bottoms are usually weighted with lead to keep them on or very near the bottom, thus preventing the escape of whatever they are being used for. For the crayfish catcher, those seines sized between six and about twelve feet are the most practical, with the smallest for singular use and the larger ones with two or three harvesters working the net. In all instances, it's a wise choice to check local laws governing the use, size, and sometimes style of seines before venturing out. Laws vary from state to state.

For the most maximum efficiency, seines should be used where they fit in best with the conditions. In other words, limit them to waters not much larger than the seine's length or width if at all possible. Small streams, ditches, and creeks are ideal spots for their use on crayfish. This assures that the fleeing crabs will not easily scuttle around the sides.

One way to put the longer nets to good use is to collect a couple of angling companions who like to use the hard shell baits as much as you. Upon entering the water of a stream, etc., have two — one on each end — anchor the seine in a half moon shape, with the seine tipped back slightly. The third crabber then enters the water upstream and starts moving back towards the net and his partners, making as much commotion along the bottom as possible. This includes such rowdy to the subsurface world behavior as tipping over rocks, kicking up debris, stirring up soft bottom, etc. This action panics the crayfish in the path of the melee, and puts them to mass flight. When they are in this state of fleeing for their lives crawdads use their tails, moving backwards with a swimming motion; and without rearview mirrors, not seeing where, either. They do so until coming across an obstruction, which in this case is the other two crabbers and the seine, which is quickly lifted by each man reaching into the water and taking hold of the submerged end first. The whole conglomeration of net, debris, and crawdads can then be carried to the bank where the crabs are sorted out. The entire process can then be repeated in another stream section if needed.

These are not the only approaches to gathering a mess of crayfish however. In the case of the tiny inch to inch and a half panfish sizes, often crabbers must look to sorting through underwater weeds and moss, along with debris piles. For this, nothing works quite as well as the same type of small net commercial bait dealers use for moving their minnows from tank to bait bucket.

In the case of regular weed growth and moss, a quick scoop through these greeneries just above where the plants meet bottom will dislodge the young claw carriers who like to cling to the plant stems and sit on the leaves if there are any.

For magnum crabs, those you could take to any self respecting lobster boil, another method works that keeps one's energy expenditures to minimum and success high by letting the crabs come to you, so to speak. It also affords the best option for where you will most likely do your best collecting, in ponds and lakes where these crustaceans seem to obtain their best growth. What the bait catcher needs is a crab trap of one sort or another.

One of the best is a converted wire mesh minnow trap whose entrance holes have been enlarged slightly. The trap can be supplied with tasty tidbits such as dead minnows, fish entrails, liver, etc. Bigger crawdads hunt food, so these freebies will get their attention.

Figure 3. For small crayfish, the bait dealer's minnow net is an indispensable tool.

The traps are placed each evening about dusk and retrieved at daybreak, or shortly thereafter. Put them in at least a couple of feet of water if possible. Otherwise, the following morning's collection may be spent looking for your trap and a furry bundle with mask who stole it. Racoons love crab legs. Well, for that matter, the rest of the crayfish too, and they have been known to actually undo the clips used on such wire traps to get at the prize inside.

Depending upon how long one wants to keep them, storing crawdads can run from simple to even simpler with a little effort. Short periods call for nothing more than placing them in damp moss or water weeds, and making use of a refrigerator to keep them cool enough to be inactive.

For periods of storage longer than a couple of days or so, a souce of oxygenated water will be needed to keep your crayfish from ending up dead bait. An aquarium and its accompanying aerator setup will work quite well, assuming that you can get away with making the goldfish disappear. The same aerator matched up with a small washtub or styrofoam cooler gives crayfish ample quarters, but make sure you secure the lid on the cooler. Wives do not usually show much enthusiasm when coming face to face with a crawdad while vacuuming or carrying in the groceries. Cats and dogs do not mind, since they make good chewies, but they end up sick and you get chewed too.

Ideally, the most optimum arrangement is to have a natural souce of freshwater such as river, lake, pond, or stream out the back door. Blessed anglers can then build a small wood and galvanized wire cage for their bait, simply keeping them in the natural habitat until use. Weighted with a few fair sized rocks, the enclosures can be used for years.

Of course, soft-shelled crabs are legend among all but the most unknowledgeable angler, and in some areas of the country, summer prices reflect this view to the max. If you are a do-it-yourselfer, you might as well make up some soft shells of your own while you're at it.

The real trick to getting a hard-shelled crayfish to a soft-shelled crab is realizing that home brewed formulas will not get the job done, but lots of food will. Crabs grow fast, from mere millimeters

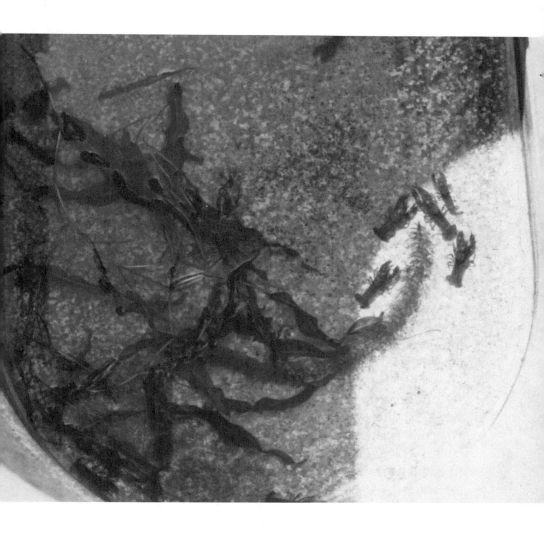

Figure 4. To make crayfish grow out of their shell give them plenty of food such as weeds, dead minnows, and the like.

at birth to inches by the end of summer in many instances. As they grow, the armor plated suit does not, hence the need to molt every so often. Simply make them grow right out of their old shells by giving them plenty of dead minnows, meat scraps, weeds, etc, while keeping them in a slightly warmer climate.

However, watch your bait mates carefully. When one of them begins to take on the telltale darkening of the shell that usually characterizes the beginnings of the molting process, remove them from the crowd. This way you will avoid another behavioral quirk of the crab family, that of the bully picking on the weak guy; and in their case making the deceased the evening meal. Also, once you start realizing efforts from your fat crab program, place the soft-shells in a refrigerator once again to retard the hardening up process that follows the growth of a new shell.

Salamanders

Most recently, salamanders are on the comeback trail as a live bait tool. Not since the early days of the Kentucky Reel have they enjoyed such popularity, which declined with the rise of multitudes of artificial baits. Anglers choosing to put these miniature dragon look alikes to use will most often find them a true big fish bait, not bothered much by juveniles, which makes them even more appealing.

In order to locate those useful to the angler, one must understand the life cycle of these amphibians. It is not the adults that you will be looking for in terms of bait, but the neotenic or gill phase, which is the intermediate state of development from hatchling to adult. Once adulthood is reached, gone are the gills and life in the water. Also, the grownups take on a sticky slime of some sort that actually seems to repel fish under most circumstances.

Two species will give the home grown bait getter his best opportunities, the Tiger Salamander and the Spotted Salamander. Both are relatively wide spread throughout the country, except for the far west. Characterized by dark bodies with bright yellow markings, the adults prefer to hang out during the warm months in moist woodlands, until winter sends them into hibernation.

Warm spring rains and temperatures bring the adults out of the no activity winter period, at which time they breed in marshes,

Juvenile (Gill Phase)

Adult Tiger

Figure 5. Salamander

low wooded areas, swamps, etc. Practically anywhere they can find a suitable puddle of water will do, as long as it's dark, secluded, and has enough H_2O. It is in such localities that the adults lay eggs, which true to amphibian form are a jelly like mass usually attached to some handy vegetation, sticks, branches, etc. Once hatched, gills intact, the young sallies live in these watering holes until either temperature and growth or the drying up of the water forces them into adulthood, and life on terra firma.

One of the ways to locate areas with salamander populations is to take a late night drive along country roads near woods, lakes, streams or other lowland areas after an evening of rain showers. If it is foggy, so much the better. These conditions bring down a great many moths and other fly by night forage, as well as drawing earthworms to the surface, providing the sallies with a veritable banquet, which they readily scurry about to take advantage of. Since moving what amounts to a block or so for us humans is akin to five miles for a sally's short legs, both breeding and living areas should be nearby.

Another wrinkle in lizard searching, which can save both time and gas, is to obtain topographic maps of the areas surrounding where a bait hunter lives. These maps, available through the U.S. Geological Survey or local natural resource departments, show lowland areas and roads that lead to them. With the maps, you can hunt the water holes in daytime looking for the telltale egg masses that upon hatching will provide you with your salamanders.

Gathering these little beasts can be done with a seine, and the aid of a friend or two, but with the normal amount of debris in the water it is not any easy task. Even easier is to take a roll of quarter inch mesh screen and form a circular cage around the egg mass, anchored by a couple of sticks to keep it formed and in place. Once the youngsters leave their eggs, you can scoop them out of the enclosure with a minnow net.

Once gotten, then they must be kept, which is not overly difficult, and really entertaining. Larger containers such as washtubs, horse tanks, aquariums, and oversized coolers are the best vessels for keeping sallies in captivity. They provide the necessary room, and allow for the addition of bits of grass, twigs, etc., to make things seem more natural. Any of these should be kept as cool as possible to prolong the neotenic stage as long as possible. Basements or root cellars are good spots, as is a refrigerator or cooler if you have access to either. You can also bury the likes of horse tanks or wash tubs in the ground, covering them with the same type of top used for your worm farming.

Feeding the young salamanders is no difficult task, since they will make a meal of just about anything they can fit into their mouths. Mayfly nymphs, small minnows, worms, mealworms, etc. will do fine. Just remember to fish out the left overs so they will not foul the container. As per normal for living things, some grow faster than others, and some tend to be a little on the me first - then you - side. This leads to some getting more than their fair share of rations, so it's a good idea to keep them more or less sorted on this basis, which will keep this problem in line.

Leeches

Leeches can be described in many ways. Ugly, disgusting, terrible, horrible, and yukky are some of the more used verbal utterages, but with PR like "The African Queen" showing the guys with suction cups at both ends draped over Bogey and Hepburn, it is no wonder. However, there are leeches and then there are leeches. All leeches that a fisherman might find use for are bloodsuckers given the chance, but are not true bloodsuckers in that they seek body fluid above all else. Rather, those that make great fish getters are primarily described as vegetarian leeches, *Erpobdellidae*, making use of decayed vegetation, tiny larvae, worms, snails, etc. In this context, these black, grey or olive drab bass, bluegill, and walleye baits differ greatly from their brightly marked parasitic relatives.

Leeches inhabit the soft, mucky bottoms of rivers, streams, ditches, ponds, lakes, and canals equally. Those anglers wishing to gather their own will find two ways to go about the business, trapping or digging. Each method is easy to accomplish, and takes a minimum of equipment and preparation.

Those desiring to trap will find that all that is required is a couple of old fine mesh onion bags, and some bloody beef or

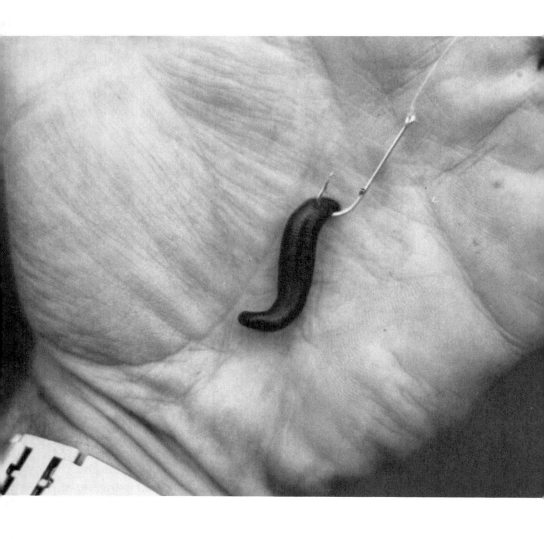

Figure 6. Vegetarian leeches, not true bloodsuckers, catch fish from bluegills to walleye.

chicken liver. The liver is placed in the used onion holders, with a small rope or heavy cord attached to the open end, and dropped into some backwater at dusk. The aroma of the bloody liver will attract the leeches to the bag, and they will attach themselves to the free meal. However, the bags must be pulled before daylight due to the wholly nocturnal nature of leeches, which sends them burrowing into the depths of the muck to escape the coming light.

The other method of harvesting leeches employs the use of either a converted coal shovel, or a bait dealer's minnow net. For waters pretty much devoid of snags, rocks, and other debris, the oversized dip net used for moving minnows from retail tank to fisherman's bucket is an ideal tool, but other waters call for hardier devices.

To make the change from shovel to leech digger or seine, a square section of the bottom of the shovel is removed with the aid of a cutting torch, or use of a drill and hack saw blade. The actual cut should run along the sides and back where the shovel begins to slope upwards, and across the front three inches from the edge all around.

Next, a series of holes are drilled completely around the cutout section approximately an inch apart and some two inches from the opening in the shovel. A piece of heavy eighth inch galvanized screen is then put in place with the aid of small screws, or pop rivets, or if one prefers, can also be welded in place. In any case, there should be no gaps left for a slippery leech to slide under the screen and escape.

Once captive, leeches are very easy to keep for months on end if desired. In order to keep activity and thus oxygen requirements to a minimum, refrigeration is a good idea. Cold temperatures in storage also keeps you from having to feed your guests. Styrofoam containers are ideal for the purpose, and water should be changed every couple of days.

If by chance the cold climatizing facilities are minimal, shade is a must when it is very warm. Some feeding will also be needed if one plans to keep leeches for a length of time under such circumstances. Liver, hamburger, etc. will all work as viable food sources, but the food should only be left in the container overnight, then removed. Otherwise, the rapid decomposition that takes place will foul the water.

Frogs

Frogs, like their amphibious cousins the salamanders, are not the prominent live bait they once were by far. Being not available under most circumstances commercially, it is wholly up to the do-it-yourself bait catcher to supply himself with these getters of fish from walleye to bass.

For the angler wishing to make use of frogs on a regular basis, finding a handy supply can be both easy and difficult. It is true that most all frogs prefer the same basic habitat, that of wet lowlands with plenty of insect life for food and cover for safety, but they sometimes do not cohabit successfully. This is especially true where the bullfrog is present in numbers.

The bullfrog, being the largest member of the frog family in the United States, is akin to a shark in the beginner's pool at the "Y", eating just about anything they care to. Regulars on the menu are salamanders, turtles, snakes, mice, small birds, crabs, insects, small fish, and ... other frogs. This last tidbit definitely places certain areas in jeopardy as far as bait supplies for the frog angler are concerned.

While the bullfrog is not a really great bait in the adult form in most areas other than the south for large-mouth, and north's musky and big pike range, three other members of the frog family do make excellent bait. Of this trio, the leopard frog is the most widespread, found across the country, with the exception of parts of the west coast. The pickerel frog joins the leopard in the east, as does the green frog. All three average out at around four inches when full grown, making them ideal for fishing.

Gathering your own frogs is almost as much fun as fishing them at times, especially when it is done with man's most basic tools, the hand. Once a near water meadow or shallow marsh is selected, all the frog hunter does is ramble around until one of the jumpers reveals his presence with a hop. Knowing where he landed, it is up to the catcher to sneak up and pounce on the catchee, technically labeled P&C by the UFC (Union of Frog Catchers). Be

sure and take a partner, (kids will do), as it alleviates the idea that you might be unhinged due to the fact that sneaking around in the weeds, mumbling blue words, and lunging every so often into the growth does appear odd to most people.

For those not inclined to such behavior, there is another way. A butterfly or fine meshed minnow net with a long enough handle will allow you to either pin the frog selected, or scoop him out of the air mid-catapult as it were. Once in the net, frogs do not hop well, lacking the necessary support.

One other way to get enough frogs for your angling expeditions is to hunt them after dark with the aid of a flashlight or headlamp, which puts the odds on the hunter for a change. The lights have somewhat of a hypnotizing effect, and the frogs most generally just set until grabbed or netted.

The only drawback to this after daylight frog stalking is that snakes are aware of the possibilities of a frog leg dinner too. It pays to carefully look around the immediate area, making sure no serpent has the same idea you do.

Keeping frogs for a prolonged length of time is an easy matter. All that is required are a container and some water. An old wash tub with a couple of inches of H_2O will do nicely, serving to keep the frogs from dehydrating, and feeling at home. An old bathtub or large cooler can be used as well, but all should be covered with screen to prevent the frogs from escape. During the warmest months, a small light bulb mounted over the container will draw lots of insects for the frogs to dine on, negating the need to worry about their nourishment.

Chapter 4

Water Borne Forage: May-Stone-Dragon and Damsel Fly Nymphs; Caddis and Helgramites

If one had to put any specific order to a listing of "natural bait", recording the various types categorically as to their fish appeal, nymphs would not and could not be far from the top. From the time freshwater species from bluegills to brook trout begin exiting the fingerling stage, these aquatic insects play a major role in food chains. Although they have departed from all but a few old time bait shops, due mostly to a lack of both knowledge and effort, in favor of commercial farm bait, nymphs will prove worth the trouble for serious bait anglers to collect. In truth, the most harassed bass or beleaguered brown trout can be plucked with the aid of a tempting water borne bait when all else has miserably failed.

Mayfly Nymphs (Wigglers)
Wigglers are most likely the premier among nymphs both name wise and use wise for live bait enthusiasts, but the label entails far more than most angler types realize. Scientifically speaking, may

Figure 8. Mayfly nymphs (wigglers) inhabit both streams and lakes, rivers and ponds in and among sand, muck, and rocks as well. A converted coal shovel makes collecting easy once their living area has been located.

flies belong to the order *Ephemeroptera*, which is made up of some 2000 known species. They inhabit both streams and lakes, rivers and ponds, in and among sand, muck, along with rocks as well. For the sake of practicality, translated ease and availability, bait catchers should direct their efforts towards gathering members of the mayfly family, *Ephemeridae*, in the eastern part of the U.S., namely *Hexagenia limbata*, or the Michigan Wiggler. These are the largest of our mayflies with average length around five eighths of an inch to an inch and a quarter, and they primarily make use of sand/clay bottoms in both lakes and rivers rather than the rock or stoney bottoms like other relatives. As for those other relatives most likely to provide a ready bait source west of the Rockies, nymphs of the family *Ephemerellidae* are the best bet from the more prevalent habitat of rapid, clear streams.

Collecting wigglers from these streams is a matter of doing it by hand upon overturning rocks and other bottom debris, much like that of gathering some crayfish; the other alternative is to place a fine wire screen against the knees while using a rake to dislodge the insects upstream, letting the force of the current push them onto the mesh and holding them in place until they can be picked off.

As for *Hexagenia*, which are burrowers living in the aforementioned bottom type, the means that bait catchers employ when after the nymph stage must include some digging to get their fish fare. Two tools, a bait dealer's minnow net or a converted coal shovel — mentioned earlier in this work — can handle this collecting chore easily once the right area has been located.

Finding wiggler beds can be very simple or a little difficult, depending on perseverance and some plain old luck at times. Naturally, the easiest way is to watch for adult hatches that lead to where the insects are dimpling the water as they lay their eggs. Keeping a check by sampling the beds to see how the immature insects are progressing through the naiad to nymph stage will let you know when to begin harvesting. This holds true for either soft bottom mayflies or the rock bound varieties, especially since the chances of coming across a different type than those two mentioned can involve nymph stages that run from six months to a year, depending on water temperature, fertilization dates and location itself.

Burrowers may be at least a little easier to find failing the sighting of adult egg layers. The soft bottom they require are most likely to be located on the inside turns of rivers and streams, and in lake areas where excessive wind does not remove debris and silt through wave action. Many times beds can be spotted by looking for the burrow holes themselves if the waters are not stained or dirty.

Two cardinal rules apply when gathering the soft bottom mayflies. First off, digging should be done from the top of mud beds down and along the edges. This means that the most mature nymphs will be encountered first, and the hatcheries will receive only slight disturbance. Rule two is that one never digs out a bed completely. It takes nature a while to put together this environment, and by leaving a base, the rebuilding process is eased. Chances are also good that later hatches of adults will repopulate these same beds if enough is there to work with, assuring bait in the future.

Once collected, wigglers can be kept for up to a couple of weeks or better if handled properly. First off, understand they are delicate. Select a styrofoam container of some sort that is long enough to allow the nymphs movement, but only place enough untreated water inside to barely cover them. Plan on changing the water daily. Add to the container enough natural aquatic vegetation to thwart the mayfly's desire to swim almost constantly once uncovered, which is natural at this stage of development. In other words, make them crawl. Otherwise, they will swim until they die from plain old exhaustion. Keeping them as cool as possible is another part of the plan to retard movement, which means using a refrigerator if at all possible.

Stonefly Nymphs

Stoneflies are certainly as important as mayflies where usable food sources for the various freshwater fishes are concerned. They have been so for at least as long too, with fossil remains dating back some 200 million years. There are almost 400 stoneflies found in the U.S. and Canada out of a thousand or so known species in the world as a whole. These *Plecoptera* insects can range from a mere eighth inch up to a couple of inches long as adults, and roughly follow the same pattern of life as the previously mentioned *Ephemeroptera*.

Figure 9. Conscientious wiggler diggers harvest from the top and edges, but never dig out a bed completely.

Without getting into an in depth classification of stoneflies, better left to those trying to pattern artificial flies on given waters, the size and home ranges of these insects afford live bait chasers options from ice fishing for panfish to big trout angling in western streams. Of more importance, is where and how to go about getting a batch in the first place to do just that. Go fishing!

Due to the fact that stoneflies require highly oxygenated and very clean water, bait harvesters must figure on doing their chores in fast running streams for the most part, although some stoneflies can be had on occasion from river riffles and wind blown — most of the time rocky — lake shore areas. That is if all of these water bodies are pollution free to a great extent.

One does not get a wide range of options when it comes to gathering stoneflies, due to these types of limited habitat, as well as the fact that they can be about as fast as a cricket at a barnyard chicken convention when things look terminal.

In most instances, the various types of stoneflies will be found utilizing such hideouts as moss or other rock clinging plant life, or under the rock itself. They also use old clam shells, logs, and other debris as well. When trying to roust them from such quarters, one will have to lift everything other than the greenery, and done with care the insects will hold on until plucked. One way to add to the odds in this respect is to leave the upstream edge of the object in place on the bottom while lifting the opposite side. This way the current flow is forced around the debris rather than hitting the insects in full force that can dislodge them. As for those living in the moss or weeds, once again a fast scooping motion through the flora with a bait net is hard to beat.

The one other method of harvesting stoneflies in an efficient manner is to use a screen in the same way as one does with crayfish or rock bound mayfly nymphs, holding it in place downstream while uprooting debris above in order to let the current wash the insects to you, and onto the screen.

Due to the delicate nature of stoneflies, and their needs in the area of oxygenation, anglers are better off collecting only enough for immediate needs. Great results when attempting to keep them for long periods should not be expected. For a few days at least, slowing them down by placing them in a refrigerator will help to a great extent, provided numbers are not so large as to cause over-crowding. Add the usual natural weed growth or bits of bottom debris to the container too.

Dragonfly Nymphs

Where the stonefly and mayfly are at least inconspicuous in either larval or adult form to many anglers, certainly the dragonfly is as outlandish, ergo obvious, with their showy colors and large size. North America plays host to some 400 species of the Odonata Order, to which damselflies are also members.

While the dragonfly nymphs are the more robust, damselflies in their nymph and adult forms are longer, slender, and seemingly more delicate. Both species are excellent underwater predators that feed on both types of nymphs already mentioned, as well as just about anything else they can overcome, including relatives. They also make use of a variety of habitat from submerged vegetation in ponds, lakes, and slow moving streams, along with debris piles of one sort or another. Some species are also burrowers much like wigglers, and have the same varying maturation periods running from a year up to five years, at which time the adults clamber ashore to transform into the even more predacious winged forms.

With like environmental preferences, these nymphs can be gathered as one would leeches or wigglers, seining the bottom muck

Figure 10. Within the 400 member Odonata Order in North America, dragonfly nymphs have proven themselves over the years as a premier live bait for do-it-yourselfers.

and debris for the burrowers. Nymphs' using old logs and other debris, can be picked by hand. Once in captivity use shallow pans or coolers with only inches of water and enough debris to keep cannibalism to a minimum.

With these large insects, the adult form, especially the dragonflies, are often an excellent bait for large panfish, bass, and trout. Capturing the adults requires the aid of the likes of a butterfly net, and a quick wrist. With their oversized eyes that can spot a mosquito a long way off, such maneuvers are a necessity. By far and away, the best collection times are late into the afternoon and early evening hours.

The adults can be kept in small cricket cages until used, with bedding such as weeds, stems, leaves, and a small tin of water for moisture. Such preparation will allow them to be held for at least a few days, but their constant need for food and life cycle does not allow them to be held too long.

Caddis Larvae
Another much appreciated nymph form to those in the fishing know that inhabits waterways across the U.S. are the various forms of caddis fly. Used properly, they will have a definite effect on creel, fish basket, and stringer weights, to the good that is.

Most of the 200 major species of caddis spend their mid-life encased in what one might call an underwater mobile home. These abodes are a combination of a special secreted silk like substance and tiny shells, twigs, pebbles, sand, and other bottom debris woven into different shapes. They take the form of tubes, shields, cylinders, and even snail shells, which makes them rather easy for bait chasers to identify, once aware of what to look for.

In swifter waters, these bug houses are attached to the underside of racks, logs, and what have you to keep them in place. Often times, after heavy rains and at night, the larvae can be spotted dragging their homes about in calmer areas as they search the bottom for bits of vegetation or other animal life to feed on.

With these kinds of looks and characteristics, caddis are relatively easy to harvest. Since they will be securely attached to many forms of debris, picking them off is a simple matter, which can be

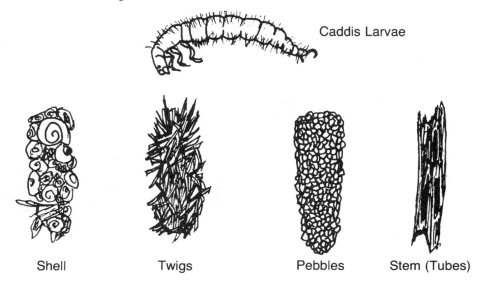

Caddis Larvae

Shell   Twigs   Pebbles   Stem (Tubes)

Figure 11. Casing Examples

done in boots or wading wet. Like dragonflies, they are very cannibalistic, so one must take the same precautions and use the same preparations if they are to be stored for any length of time. When it is time to place them on a hook, simply squeezing the rear end of the debris they have molded will force the head out long enough to get a grip and remove the larvae from the casing.

Helgramites

Helgramites, as the nymph form of the Dobson Fly, are without much doubt the best river and stream smallmouth bass bait around. Unfortunately, they are also the least common of just about all of the nymph forms due to urbanization, pollution, channelization, and other man made blights.

Helgramites spend their almost three seasons as a nymph in the swifter portions of rivers and streams clinging to the underside of rocks with the small pincers at the end of their tail. The only really practical way to harvest these creatures is to use a rake and screen in the same manner as with other nymphs such as stoneflies. The only difference in the entire procedure is that the screen should be no further than eighteen inches from those rocks being over-

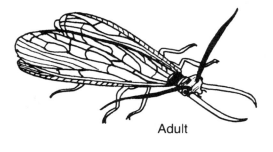
Adult

Larvae (Nymph)

Figure 12. Helgramite (Dobson Fly)

turned. This will prevent the large, powerful helgies from grabbing onto something other than the screen, which they can do quickly when disturbed.

It would also be wise to inject a word of warning at this stage, concerning the handling of these nymphs. The helgramites, due to their very proficient predatory lifestyle, are equipped with a large set of mandible jaws or pincers at the front end, in addition to those smaller ones at the rear already mentioned. These jaws are very powerful, and capable of inflicting one heck of a bite, given the opportunity, so it pays to avoid them.

Unlike some other nymphs, helgramites will keep very well in several types of environment. Perhaps one of the better ways if possible is to store them in an aquarium away from direct sunlight to keep the water cooler. In addition, they will also hold well in a shallow pan or cooler setup as long as the water is aerated.

The third way to store Dobson Fly larvae is placing them in some type of box or styrofoam bucket along with damp moss or wet leaves. Put into the refrigerator, they can be held in such a manner for some time, perhaps weeks. In any, and all cases, where anglers plan to make use of helgramites, plan on feeding them a bit of hamburger to keep their ravenous appetites from getting the best of the population.

Chapter 5

Fishy Fish Food: Minnows

If there is one type of live bait that rivals the nightcrawler and his cousins for first place among the live breathing bait fraternity, it is minnows. In fact, at certain times of the year, or for particular species, and specific locales, they may even out-do the worm family.

The minnow group is indeed a large one, encompassing around 2000 species with some 192 members in the United States alone, ranging from baitfish in the two inch bracket to carp well over the fifty pound mark. Naturally, a fifty pound carp does not make the most desirable baitfish. Casting one would be difficult for mere mortals. Facts like that in conjunction with natural distribution, population levels or the plain old familiarity of one species over another means some minnows are far more suited to the do-it-yourself bait getters than others.

Chubs

Included under the commonly used label, "Chub", anglers are likely to run across the Creek, Lake, Silver, and Redtail or Hornyhead Chubs. Local handles notwithstanding, all share the com-

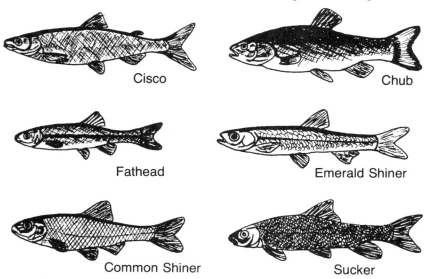

Cisco   Chub

Fathead   Emerald Shiner

Common Shiner   Sucker

Figure 13. Minnow Species

mon traits of preferring clean-clear waters with plenty of oxygen
and cool temperatures whether it be river, lake, or stream.

Probably the most popular among this branch of the baitfish
family is the Redtail or Hornyhead, distributed from Wyoming to
the East Coast, and south to Alabama and Arkansas. *Hybopsis
bigutatta* acquire their name from a reddish orange tail and the small
horn like growths on the male's head during spawn time. Other
identifying marks include a dark spot at the base of the tail, and a
thick body with large head and very distinct scale pattern. Redtails
are tough on the hook, and all size ranges from juvenile to adult
provide live baiters the means to catch everyting from crappie to
musky.

Very similar to the redtails are Creek Chubs, often confused
with their cousins enough to completely change identities among
most fishermen. Their natural range, which runs from southern
Canada across the U.S. with the exception of the West Coast and
some west-central states also overlaps that of the Hornyheads, which
does not help.

Semotilus atromaculatus is a bit smaller on the average though
more round in appearance, and is more silvery than the dark olive

cast of the redtails. Creek Chubs also seem to prefer smaller brooks and streams than than those of their red relatives.

The Lake Chub is a more restricted member of this baitfish clan, inhabiting waters from southern Canada to Iowa and Michigan. Average size for these minnows is around three inches, making them ideal for the likes of smallmouth and walleyes, and they are slim as well with a greyish lateral line running across silver-blue sides. The scientific label for the Lake Chub is *Hybopsis plumbea*.

Silver Chubs, *Hybopsis storeriana*, are another weight watcher minnow, long and slim with a greenish back and silver belly. Found from central Canada south to Alabama and Oklahoma and all parts in between. Silvers can reach ten inches at times and do well after capture, which makes these a good bet for bait getters.

Finally, there is one other prominent member of this foragefish family, *Hybopsis micropogon*, called River Chub by most anglers. River chubs can grow to a foot long, which makes them one of the larger baitfish. Ranging from the Rockies to New England and south to Alabama, they often create havoc with many trout stream anglers after the more glamorous salmonoids. These chubs also resemble other members of the family with a blunt face and large body, but coloration makes the difference in identification with olive-brown sides intermingled by single or doubled dark scale patches over a cream belly, somewhat resembling a camouflage pattern.

Shiners

Shiners are more widely known in most areas these days, compared to the chubs, simply because in some cases they are widely raised commercially. There are other members of the family however, who do far better in the wild state, meaning that it's up to the get-your-own angler, if he wants them in his bait bucket at all.

Notemigonus crysoleuces, which is a toothful, also goes by the much easier mouthed names "Pond Shiner", or "Goldy". Juvenile fish usually end up being more silver than gold until older, but all exhibit the characteristic wide body. Golden shiners prefer lakes and ponds over rivers as a whole, choosing to hang out near weedbeds in rather large schools. While originating from southern

Canada and the Eastern U.S. south to Mexico, in recent years, this baitfish through commercialization has been introduced to many waters west of the Rocky Mountains.

Common shiners, or just "shiner", which is the name most often used, are not so readily propagated as golden shiners, most likely due to their need for heavily oxygenated waters like those of rivers and streams. Although a deep bodied baitfish like goldies, they are slightly less robust, growing up to eight inches in length at times, and exhibiting a bright silver coloration in both adult and juvenile phases. *Notropis cornutis* is generally found at home from East of the Rockies to the Atlantic Coast and north to Canada.

Another member of the shiner family, Emeralds, get their name honestly from a light green emerald tone back over silver sides. Thin and delicate, these baitfish prefer the clearest of waters, be they lake or stream. Although emeralds do not exceed four inches usually, they can grow up to five, and are known for being a fish of suspension during daylight hours. After dark is another matter, as these baitfish move nearer to the surface in search of plankton and midget insects to dine on. General locations for the emerald shiner run from Texas to Canada, and they are a steady forage for most game and some panfish. Their scientific name is *Notropia atherinoides*, and like the common shiners they do not take well to commercial effort.

Spottail shiners are one of the smaller members of the shiner tribe, preferring waters like those of the emerald, clear and clean. Rarely do they exceed five inches. Their home range includes the Dakotas and the area to the Hudson River, south to Virginia then back west to Iowa. Spottails, *Notropis hudsonius*, are extremely silver in color with a distinct spot at the base of the caudal or tail fin, hence their common name.

There are other baitfish species that can often fit the bill of those anglers wishing to harvest their own, and subsequently fish them as well. One of the most widely distributed of these is the Fathead Minnow.

Pimphales promelas seldom gets any larger than three inches, and varies in color from olive green to almost black. Fond of bog lakes, and slow streams, and ponds in the north; silty bottom lakes

and like streams in the south, fatheads are a prolific lot. For this reason, and their toughness to adverse conditions as a whole, they are part of a commercial industry as large as that of the goldies. That fact is responsible in great part for their being found throughout the U.S. and southern Canada, making them useful for everything from perch to pickerel and a very viable option for bait anglers.

Sucker minnows are another group of baitfish worth the effort on occasion. In larger sizes, they make excellent fare for the likes of big musky and northerns, while smaller sizes can be used for brown trout, smallmouth bass, and channel catfish. There are numerous members of the sucker clan, among them the White Sucker, Silver Redhorse, Lake Chubsucker, and others. Although not thought of as such since they are bottom feeders by trade, suckers are generally fish of clear, clean lakes and streams for the most part. With such a large family, suckers are likely to be found by bait hunters in all parts of the country in one form or another.

The Bluntnose Minnow, *Hyborhynchus notatus*, is common to clear lakes and smaller streams throughout the Great Lakes area, south to Virginia and into the Gulf states. A small minnow, silver with a darkened lateral line and blunt face, they are most notably located around docks, piers, and other manmade structures on such waters if they exist. They take easily with either net or trap, and being no bigger than four inches maximum, ideal for panfish, and small bait loving gamefish.

Harvesting & Storing Methods

Getting your own baitfish is usually most efficiently handled by two means, trapping or seining. On occasion however, when a quick supply is needed, larger minnows such as suckers, chubs, and shiners can also be taken with hook and line. Cane or telescoping fiberglass poles do the trick nicely, with a light shot and small hook baited with grubs or red worms. Once the rap of an interested party is felt, a simple lift of the pole will hook and lift the minnow from the water all in one motion to the waiting bucket. A reeling fight that can injure the minnow or spooking of the school through the commotion is thus avoided.

Proper use of the other methods in turn is not just simply

throwing a trap in the water or scurrying about for a quick scoop with the seine. Each species have their little quirks to consider when one harvests. This also goes for keeping minnows after you get them.

Chubs

As mentioned previously, chubs like clear-clean water, which translates to the fact that they can afford to be very wary, and will spook at the slightest disturbance. Always approach an area slowly from downstream, and never drop buckets, trap, seine if at all possible. Bank vibrations are deadly tipoffs that something big is on the prowl.

Whether seining or trapping, the best locations are those out of the way spots on a stream or river that attract little human traffic. Failing that, plan on doing the harvesting very early or late in the day when activity is minimal. Seining calls for at least two people working an eight foot or larger net if local law allows it. Smaller streams should be worked so that one man is downstream of the other close to the bank. Meanwhile, the other can wade out and upstream, net outstretched, then move back towards the bank, creating a "v" with the bank being the other leg, that collapses. Walking towards shore thus will effectively trap the minnows between net and bank as they use the current to speed them downstream in an effort to escape.

The hardest part of trapping chubs is locating the prime holding spots in any given stream. These baitfish prefer a little faster current than shiners, with riffles or spots along the edges of weed patches-large rocks-logs where current is funneled, carrying with it the food these minnows prefer. Both glass and wire traps will work on chubs, but it will take more time for them to get used to the wire in populated areas. It helps if the wire is either discolored from age or painted to match the bottom, and plan on letting the trap alone for a couple of hours at least, baited with bread crumbs or oatmeal, funnel downstream.

Keeping chubs for any length of time calls for some preparation. Small fish should never be placed with larger ones who will dine on them given the chance, cannibals that they are. Horse tanks

Figure 15. Aeration for minnows can be provided by pet store bellows type agitators.

filled with rain or other strictly natural water are ideal. Aeration can be provided by either a commercial bait dealer's agitator or the pet store bellows pump variety.

For those anglers planning to keep no more than a dozen or so minnows in the medium to small size range for a short time only, a thirty gallon aquarium setup works very well. The initial cost of such is not what you would call cheap, but at today's baitfish prices of twenty-five cents up apiece, it does not take long for the glass tanks to pay for themselves.

In either case, chubs can be fed small bits of worm, bread and oatmeal, or grubs to sustain them for a longer period of time. The trick is to not overdo it in the amounts placed in the containers. That way, there is no decomposition of unused food that can lead to less oxygen and disease, which is also the prime reason for removing dead baitfish as soon as they are discovered. In outside tanks, there will be some algae growth, but that is not a major problem since the baitfish will utilize such as an added food source.

Shiners

Shiners seem to be a bit more delicate than chubs, hence the need for added care in both the harvesting and holding of these baitfish. Although seining is an alternative, shiners are better off being trapped. Glass traps seem to produce more than wire, perhaps because the struggles of previously entrapped minnows appears as though they were in a feeding frenzy through the distortion of the glass. Minnows epitomize monkey see-monkey do when it comes to food.

Shiners do not inhabit quite the same water as that of chubs either, preferring current that is a bit slower. This makes their holding areas easier to spot for bait catchers wishing to find a place to locate a trap. Baiting is the same however, using dry bread crumbs, oatmeal, or crushed-unsalted crackers. One nice thing about the oatmeal though is that it milks with the current, often drawing fish from downstream as they follow the trail to the trap.

As for Goldies, while not what you would call tough they do hold up a little better than their silver cousins, except when found in shallow ponds and lakes during the heat of summer. At this time they tend to be bruise prone, and should also be trapped rather than netted. When you can use the seine, one trick to getting a bunch at one whack is to ball up some oatmeal and toss it in. Once the goldies gather for lunch, two men can sneak into the water, wade out deeper, then come at them from the back side, and like chubs in the creek, pin them against the shoreline. Stealth is the key, along with them supplying the gluttony.

For storing, horse tanks and aquariums are the way to go with these species also. Outside, you can create your own self-service feeding station by placing a dim bulb over the tanks. Dusk and dawn will see a great many insects attracted to the light, only to fall into the water. The shiners will readily rise to pick them off as they do.

Emerald and Spottail Shiners

Both emerald and spottail shiners, along with bluntnose, are captured the easiest from around docks and piers on lakes with sand or gravel bottoms, although at different times. A square net with metal arms that fold out to resemble the framework of an umbrella is one way to do it. The umbrella seine (net) as it is called, is placed in the water where it quickly settles to the bottom. Squatting, so as to keep a low profile, the catcher then tosses out a batch of crumbs or oatmeal that hopefully settles to the bottom squarely in the middle of the net. By the way, use old bread since the new stuff floats like a cork in a bottle.

Remain motionless and avoid a shadow until sufficient numbers of baitfish are moving into or actually feeding in the net. Then, with as fast a motion as able lift the net straight up and out of the water. The aid of a stout pole in the six to eight foot range will provide enough leverage, tied to the rope attached in turn to the ring on top of the net frame. That will take care of acquiring a batch of spottails or bluntnoses, but the emeralds must be dealt with in a different time frame; after dark, and over open water too.

Once darkness arrives, those rising schools of plankton that the emeralds use as forage are readily attracted to light. Anglers enlisting the aid of either spotlight or lantern can do just that, drawing the microscopic animals boatside, followed by the hungry shiners.

The light is hung over the side of the boat so that it shines directly into the water. Use reflectors with a lantern. With a spot, run off a twelve volt battery, you can also mount it in an innertube thus floating it right on the water. The net is then suspended a couple or three feet below the surface. Once baitfish start buzzing back and forth through the light beam in pursuit of a meal, you can haul away anytime you feel the numbers sufficient.

I should also add that spottail and bluntnose shiners lend them-selves to capture with glass traps too. Set up in the same manner as with stream trapping. Large numbers can be had this way, especially in the spring of the year when they first invade the shallows.

Bluntnose, emeralds, and spottails do not really do well in captivity so it is generally preferable to seine or trap only what you need for the present, assuring that you will not kill off any more than is necessary during the course of normal use.

Fatheads and suckers are another matter. Both can be kept for quite a while, especially at both ends of the year when things are cool enough to slow down their metabolism. Fathead can be harvested by either method with little effort, but suckers do not come to a trap at all well. For numbers of them, seining is a far better option.

Chapter 6

Land Born Forage:
Crickets, Hoppers, & Catalpa Worms

The ingredients of this chapter could just as well be titled, "Panfishermen's Favorites" since the above trio is responsible for boatload after boatload of little skillet fitters every year that anglers get their bait wet. What also makes them appealing is that they are readily available in an uncommercial state for the fisherman who doubles on the side as his own bait catcher.

Crickets are the noisy ones of the bunch who hang under bedroom windows serenading on hot summer nights. The two most common species of field crickets that serve live baiters well are the grays and black crickets. During daylight hours, they can most often be found hiding around foundations, outbuildings, field edges, and lumber piles left relatively undisturbed for long periods of time. In town, they seek homes under garbage cans, along sidewalk edges, and the like. In short, one can find them just about anywhere you care to look.

Crickets can be gathered in a couple of ways, the most common among schoolboys and adventurer types being to lift or tip rocks, boards, trash cans and what have you, grabbing as many as possible before they scatter. For us older— wiser not lazier— bait chasers, there is a much easier way, that also proves to be more efficient, thus reputation saving.

First of all, in the way of materials, you need to round up a couple of dozen or so discarded cardboard rolls from paper towels, aluminum foil, wax paper or t.p. For the uninitiated that happens to be toilet paper, which is the most abundant of all, especially if one has kids around. They go through the stuff faster than ice cream at an oven convention, averaging what seems like a roll a day.

The empty rolls are then waterproofed by brushing melted wax on the outside, or they can be taped or painted as well. Next up is to seal one end either with a plastic lid of some sort if you can find one that fits, or tape it also. Plugs can also be made by wadding up a piece of cloth or paper and shoving them inside.

The rolls are baited with bits of apple, old bread, lettuce, chicken feed, or cereal, and scattered in different locations around a field, or weedy vacant lot. In order to make them appear as natural as possible, and keep them from being picked up by a curious soul, they should also be partially covered with bits of grass, some leaves, or whatever else is handy.

In a day or so, collection is as easy as going around to each bait station and emptying the contents into a container. The traps are then re-baited and put back in place or moved to a new location.

Keeping crickets can be a delicate operation, depending on the time of year, and how you deal with their extremely cannibalistic nature. Fresh food and water should be present at all times to lessen the latter as much as possible. During periods when the weather can sneak in an unexpected frost, they should be kept inside the garage, or basement if possible.

Crickets will eat just about anything from your wife's new curtains to the kid's breakfast cereal, so feeding is not a big problem. However, certain food items other than normally dry chicken feed and cereal will sour. Things such as lettuce, apples, and the like will have to be replaced frequently.

The big mistake that many cricketeers make is not making enough fresh water available for their insects. The ideal cricket watering trough is the discarded lid from a small jar such as jelly. They are shallow enough so that adult crickets can fall in should they get careless and still not drown, yet they will hold enough water for about fifty crickets for a couple of days. The lids should be cleaned and the water changed more often if it gets dirty.

There are a great many containers that crickets can be held in until they go fishing. Some of the better ones are clean garbage cans, wash tubs, and those five gallon plastic buckets that restaurants get their cooking grease or lard in. In the case of the metal containers, the top five or six inches should be sanded smooth and waxed. Otherwise, the expert climbing crickets will be able to crawl out without too much trouble.

You can also keep crickets in homemade cages, which are ideal for large numbers of the chirpers. Most cages are made from plywood and window screen with circular holes cut in the top for easy access of a hand. For cleaning, it also helps to hinge the entire top section so that it can be lifted up. The holes are fitted with half a coffee can, or something similar in size. Slid down into the plywood, the cans keep crickets from getting near the open holes and freedom. Another way to do it is by nailing a piece of rubber innertube across the opening, then slit it just enough so that you can get your hand in.

Bedding material for prolonged storage varies as much as what the keeper has on hand at the time. Old egg cartons, split in half, are fine. So are the very same paper rolls used in trapping the insects, crumpled newspaper, grass, leaves, and bits of old rag, as well as shredded packing paper. In all cases, the bedding should be changed at least every other week, both for the cricket's sake and yours, since the odor of old crickets is to say the least, pungent.

Grasshoppers

The types of fish grasshoppers will catch, vary as much as the different sizes and types of hoppers themselves. Larger hoppers will get catfish and bass by the bunch, medium size are terrific for trout, and the small sizes are just right for perch, crappies, and bluegills. Grasshoppers can even be frozen alive and used in the winter for ice fishing.

Figure 16. Coffee can halves, inserted in cage tops, keep crickets from getting near the opening and climbing out to freedom. Early mornings are an easy time to collect grasshoppers from their stem beds.

The biggest problem for the angler who wants to round up a few dozen "Piston Legs" for a day on the lake or stream is just that. The capture! There are several methods that might enable one to accomplish this, some easier than others. Butterfly nets work fairly well, as do outsized fly swatters, which are used to pin the insects to the ground rather than bop them. Another way that is much easier on the old ticker and legs employs the aid of several old pair of pantyhose.

First, take the hose and cut them where the legs meet the panty portion, then split each leg from toe to top. Next, select two 1x2 inch boards that have been cut to a point on one end, and staple each section of hose strip first to one board then the other. Outstretched, you now have a first rate grasshopper net. Upon selecting an area with an ample supply of hoppers, usually a field or vacant lot with plenty of tall weeds, stretch out the hose and push or hammer each stake into the ground just enough so that it will stand by itself.

By walking up to the outstretched hose in a slow, deliberate manner, the hoppers will be forced from their hiding places in the weeds, taking to the air or jumping to get out of your way. When they land on the hose, their barbed legs will become snarled in the nylon fiber, prohibiting any further progress. For the bait catcher, it is then a relatively simple matter to pluck the grasshoppers off the net and drop them in a container.

A way that is just as easy entails taking advantage of both the grasshopper's sleeping habits and Mother Nature at the same time. During the summer and early autumn, when hoppers are most abundant and their activity the greatest, air temperatures and humidity are both high during the daylight hours. As evening arrives, the temperatures drop off, but the humidity either stays the same or even rises.

Hoppers climb the tallest weeds in the evening to spend the night in relative safety from ground crawling predators such as spiders, salamanders, and toads. Taking this into consideration, and the fact that lower temperatures and high humidity put the grasshoppers in somewhat of a semi-dormant state, means that it is very easy to take an early morning walk collecting hoppers with little trouble. Until the sun gets high enough to warm them up, they will cling to their stem bed in the most docile manner.

Once you get them, successfully keeping hoppers is not much different from keeping crickets. The same type of containers will do the job, but you must keep can types covered with screen. With the least bit of leverage, they will vault the top for sure otherwise. If wood cages are used, be sure to use the innertube top only. Activity can also be decreased greatly by placing the container in a darkened basement or covering it with a black cloth to simulate night.

The best bedding material is the same weeds that the hoppers came from, making them feel most at home and providing a ready made food supply as well. As for watering, their requirements are the same as crickets also, and you can use jelly lids for troughs once more.

Catalpa Worms

The larvae of the Sphinx Moth is considered by many an old panfish hand as "the" premier bait for mid-summer bluegills, and they do not do too bad on bass, catfish, and perch either. Besides being a very eye pleasing blend of black-white-yellowgreen, they are very sturdy on the hook as well, capable of producing up to as many as a half dozen fish per worm.

Catalpa worms spend approximately half their life cycle in the trees from which they glean their common name. They begin life as an egg which has been laid on the catalpa tree leaves by the previous generation of moths, which soon after expire. Upon hatching, they become furious eating machines which devour leaf after leaf until they reach a length of around three inches. At that time, they are too fat to hang onto the foliage any longer and drop to the ground where they burrow into the soil to pupate, hatching into adults the following spring.

Finding a grove of catalpa trees that have worms, but have not seen other do-it-yourselfers is the biggest problem. There are bait dealers, both wholesale and retail, who rent these groves by the tree every year to insure an unmolested and adequate supply for their customers. When a catalpa hunter goes out, he or she should take "the find" home with them, unless looking to go hunting for new trees to harvest the following summer.

Anglers can usually start looking for hatched out worms as early as mid-June in the northern areas, much earlier down south, depending on the year's weather. Cool temps may retard things by as long as several weeks, and many times a heavy wind or rain storm will wipe out an entire hatch, often leaving the tree or trees barren for a year or two.

Sophisticated equipment is not a must, nor even remotely required in order to get a mess of worms for fishing. Any five gallon bucket or pail will do the trick for a picking and transport vessel. However, a large washtub or box, either of wood or cardboard should be waiting either at the car or at home. The reason for such is that you will need something large to store all the leaves you must have on hand in order to keep the worms for a while.

When harvesting, since the worms are already on the leaves eating their lives away, it is a waste of time to pick them off one by one. Much simpler and quicker is to just break off the entire leaf at the base on the branch, and drop it in the bucket. In order to get at those leaves and worms out of reach from the ground or a ladder, you might consider acquiring a pruning tool from the local garden tool supply store. You can also make one from a couple of old broom handles fastened to a pair of scissors, which will cut leaf stems easily.

Naturally, some of the worms will be smaller than others who hatched a few hours to a day earlier, but this is of no real concern since they will eat and grow as long as fresh leaves are supplied. Most of the time this works out better anyway, insuring a continuing maturing supply as well as having on hand some smaller worms on those days the fish seem to want it that way.

There is only one other thing that a catalpa hunter need be worried about, and this is the predation of his stock by wasps. The wasps do not actually kill the larvae right off, but actually lay their eggs on the backs of the worms instead. It is the young wasp pupae that kill the larvae by sucking the interior juices from them as sustenance for themselves. So, when harvesting the catalpa worms be on the lookout for any white tube shaped sacks attached to the worm's back. These should be removed at once, and if possible put these to use first. Also, check your stocks at home every other day or so for the same as new hatches of the wasp eggs may occur.

Chapter 7

Oddball & Miscellaneous Bait

Usable bait does not just stop with the "Name Brands" known so well by most angler types. There are other oddball varieties of various chewies that offer the do-it-yourself bait collector a chance to get something new wet once in a while. Off beat baits can also tip the odds in the fisherman's favor on occasion, especially after a piece of water, and the inhabitants thereof, have been over-worked by more standard forms of natural fish catchers.

Maggots

One of the easiest and most useful, although certainly not the most glamorous, of these baits for everything from panfish to trout is the maggot. The uptown name is spikes. In real terms, spikes are nothing more than the larval stage of flies, be they blue or green bottle variety, or larger carrion flies.

The adult insects lay their eggs on just about anything long gone from the mortal coil — decomposing material — that is handy from vegetables to dead animals. When the eggs hatch, the tiny larvae begin feeding on the material at hand, growing rapidly until they reach around a half inch in length. At this time, they crawl off to begin pupation as a brown cocoon until developing into another generation of adult flies. Timing of such development depends on the temperature range, which can mean only a few days in mid-summer to a week in cooler times. Unless indoors, no activity occurs during the winter.

The most sanitary method of acquiring a ready supply of spikes is to use whole fish, such as carp or suckers — perhaps the leftovers from other fish cleaning chores if so inclined. The cadavers or remains are simply laid out on a pine board that has been screened off on three sides to allow only one exit for those maggots attempting to crawl off when large enough. The board is suspended above ground on a two by four, or like post, to keep racoons, possums, and the neighbor's prized pussycat from getting at the fish. Below the platform, a shallow pan large enough to extend beyond the board edge is placed. Filled about mid-depth with cornmeal, the maggots will burrow right in, cleaning themselves in the process.

Since it may not take too long for the spikes to pupate, daily sifting of the material is a good idea, once you begin to see mature larvae on the carcasses atop the platform. Then, in order to arrest the process, the fly larvae can be placed in a container with fresh cornmeal, and set in a refrigerator until time to head for the lake. Holding them for a month or more this way is not uncommon. In a heated outbuilding, bait chasers can guarantee themselves a supply all winter if they are inclined. The flies will keep doing their part as long as they are kept warm enough.

Wasp Larvae

The larval stages of either Mud Dauber or Paper wasps are still another little used bait form that is reliable in filling a fish sack. Of course, one must be smart enough to get past the very protective adults of the Paper Wasp species.

Bait chasers can find the stem suspended nest of the paper wasps hanging under eaves troughs, in old barns and other outbuildings, as well as trees. Once located, coming back after dark in the warm months is the most sensible way to get the bait and avoid getting stung. If possible, try to pick a night when humidity levels are high. Wasps do not fly well at night and airborne moisture

Figure 17. The larval stages of either Mud Dauber or Paper Wasps are a little used but reliable bait form for filling fish sacks.

keeps them even more incapacitated. So much so that with the aid of a broom, they can be swept off the nest if outdoors, or the entire nest knocked down if they are all inside for the evening.

Once on the ground, a thorough dowsing with a bucket of water or the hose if handy will make sure they do not put one in much danger. After that, put on a pair of heavy rubber gloves and split the nest, picking up the adult stingers and tossing them aside. Remove the larval chambers and store.

Mud dauber larvae is by far easier to come by since the females leave their egg and subsequent larvae to develop on its own. Once the egg is laid in a chamber constructed of mud, food stuffs are added in the way of paralyzed spiders, and the dirt incubator sealed. When the larvae hatches, breakfast is waiting, and the juvenile wasps feed and grow until they are old enough to break out of the chamber. These mud nests can be spotted on the sides of rafters, walls, and overhangs of garages, barns, and other outbuildings.

There is only one place to keep either type of wasp larvae, that being in the safety of a refrigerator. This way, anglers can rest assured that they will not be privileged to witnessing first hand the results of progression from egg to bad-tempered adults when they least expect it. As for containers, old milk or cream cartons, cottage cheese cups, or even plastic bags like the ones used to pack lunches in will do for holding larvae until it is time to go fishing.

Cockroaches

The scourge of the restaurant and kitchen is one of the finer summer bluegill and crappie baits, and they can do their fair share at times in the winter as well. Cockroaches generally hide out in cool, dark places during the daylight hours, foraging at night.

Roaches can be raised or trapped to use for bait, and if they are not native to your dwellings, the latter would be the better suggestion to avoid them becoming permanent residents and neighbors. The same type of paper towel roll trap used for crickets will do on roaches as well. They should be placed under sinks, cabinets, and other darkened-damp locations for maximum success. Bait should include bits of bread and vegetables such as lettuce or celery.

For those inclined to attempt raising these fast runners, a metal garbage can with its bottom lined with straw or excelsior will do fine. Food stuffs can include the same items used in the trapping, along with fruit or a mixture of whole wheat flour, skim milk, and brewer's yeast mixed in a 50/40/10 ratio respectively. Like crickets too, roaches require a good deal of water so do-it-yourselfers should make use of the same type of lid watering troughs, replenished frequently.

Freshwater Shrimp

These tiny freshwater relatives of the large ocean shrimp are a delicacy to many members of the panfish family, and are relished by stream trout and smallmouth as well. Although used frequently in the southern U.S., anglers elsewhere for the most part do not take advantage of them.

Freshwater shrimp are found around the bases of soft bottom weedgrowth, and in mudbanks along with nymphs, wigglers, and other aquatic life. Since they are rather delicate, the best method of harvesting is to employ the same type of coal shovel tool used in digging wigglers, only a finer screen should be substituted because the crustaceans will seldom be larger than half an inch long.

Freshwater shrimp are not likely to be raised in captivity, so hunting is the only way to obtain supplies for fishing needs. Once in the bucket, anglers should also add plenty of weed growth to keep them from scurrying about until exhaustion causes death. Storing in a refrigerator will help retard this to some degree, and will also diminish the need for oxygen.

Corn Borers & Horseweed Worms

These two individuals are a case of one bait with two names, each being favored at different times of the year. If that sounds confusing, it probably is. The European Corn Borer is a great bait for ice fishing, and a scourge to farmers from the Rockies eastward. Control of these pests, which are the larvae of the Maize Moth, is difficult because they inhabit wild plants other than corn, one of which happens to be commonly called "Horseweed". That is where the name "Horseweed Worm" gets into the act. Weed worms have long been a favorite of summer anglers. Ah, the light begins to get brighter. In other words, use the bait any time you can get your hands on some.

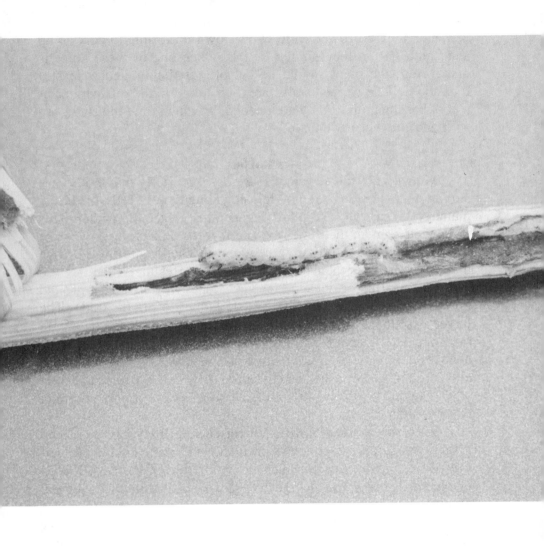

Figure 18. Clipped stalks that hold borers can be stored in basements or a refrigerator until they are needed for fishing.

Since these borers are interior feeders of the stalks of growing plants, it is impractical to raise them. To find productive stalks of either corn or horseweed in the field, those harboring larvae, each stalk will have to be examined for small entry holes made by the larvae as they burrowed in to chow down until time to cocoon up and hatch late in the summer or fall. Once one of these holes is discovered, the plant should be cut off just below and at least a foot above. The clipped stalks are then stored in the refrigerator or a cool basement until they are needed, at which time the stalks are split and the worms removed.

Mousies

Mousies are the larvae of *Eristalis tenax*, a fly that looks very similar to a honey bee, not related though, but feeds on liquid manure, rotten fruit, and other degenerative vegetable matter. This fly lays its eggs in the same material it feeds on and the grey/white larvae make use of it in the same manner. The long tail-like device that gives mousies their name is actually a breathing tube.

Cattle farms, fruit canneries, and places where silage is ground up are all prime areas for the mousie hunter to ply his trade. The larvae is scooped up along with the material, and placed on a wire screen rack. Using either hose or bucket, water is employed to rinse away excess material until the grubs are revealed. As for scooping, either a bait dealer's net or cut out shovel will do fine, and it is advisable that one wears at least knee boots unless you like burning clothes often.

Once the mousies have been rinsed free, they can be placed in old cottage cheese containers which have been filled about half full of fine sawdust or cornmeal, or a mixture of the two. Placed in the refrigerator, the larvae will go dormant for up to several months at least.

Given the facilities, mousies lend themselves to raising very well. Material such as liquid manure can be obtained, or you can make your own using some squashed tomatoes with just a little water added. Both mediums can be placed in either a wash tub or small horse tank, depth being from 3-5 inches. Keep the liquid shaded from the sun so it will not dry out through evaporation, and

Figure 19. Waste material like this liquid manure is the place to scoop mousies.

check daily to see if flies are working the material. Once discovered, a screen can be placed over the container, imprisoning the adults in order to make sure that egg laying will be there and not somewhere else.

In all but sub-freezing temperatures, the material will keep producing larvae since it is heating as it breaks down. If in an outbuilding that is heated, the process can be kept going over the winter, providing an excellent ice fishing bait as long as the adults are warm enough to keep egg laying.

Mealworms

Mealworms are the larvae of the Darkling Beetle, and come in both a yellow and dark color phase. They not only fill a niche as a popular panfishing bait, but are also a major food source for pet and aquarium shops in order to feed both birds and fish.

The beetles and their subsequent larvae are most often found naturally in graineries and poultry houses where significant amounts of grain are stored. Since they do a great deal of damage to said grain stocks, the owners and operators will usually be happy to allow someone to gather as many larvae as they wish. On the other hand, anglers need not really make more than one trip to such places, if they choose to do so in the hopes of gathering some breeders for home raising, which is not a difficult task.

Equipment needed for raising mealworms consists of a washtub, a piece of fine wire screen large enough to cover the tub, a good supply of chicken mash, and four or five pieces of old burlap. First of all, a quarter inch layer of mash is poured into the tub, followed by a piece of the burlap laid over it. The procedure is repeated until all layers of burlap and mash are in the tub. Then, the breeder beetles are placed inside, and a few carrots or potatoes are added to provide moisture. A daily sprinkling of water is required so as to keep the mixture dampened.

The adult beetles will move about the layers, feeding and depositing their eggs, which will soon hatch. When the larvae is from a half to three quarters of an inch long, they are ready to be harvested. Cottage cheese containers make good storage cups to which around three dozen mealworms should be added. Filled about half way with mash, they can then be put into the refrigerator until use.

Madtoms

Madtoms are not a bait for the squeamish nor the clumsy. They can inflict a painful sting, and some people are even allergic to the toxin from the horned fins of these little catfish. However, they are indeed an excellent live bait for such species as walleye, smallmouth bass, other catfish, and even pike on occasion.

Madtoms are actually the juveniles of bullheads when they are in the 1-3 inch size range, as well as being members of the yellow catfish family. Either black or yellow bullheads can fit the bill for the bait catcher as well, which in their case, dictates where one has to look.

Blacks are the least choosy as to where they live, often inhabiting waters that are less than clean, very sluggish and muddy. After dark, small groups of the baby cats can be found cruising in very shallow water, once the entire hatch of an adult pair has taken place. The easiest way to gather them is to walk or wade these areas with a fine mesh net and headlight, scooping up the young cats as they turn up in the light beam.

Yellow bullheads prefer a cleaner habitat than that of the blacks. Although they can be found in moderately flowing sections of rivers and streams, fast waters are not their forte. In this regard, they are like the yellow catfish, which prefers spending daylight hours under small rocks and in heavy weedgrowth that shields them from the sun. Such a hard bottom environment makes it easy for bait catchers to get at them by wading during the daytime.

When these young cats are found under rocks, the easiest way to corral them is with the aid of a three pound coffee can that has both ends removed. By slowly lifting the rock, anglers quite often can avoid spooking the little cats laying on the bottom, slip the can into place then net the baitfish. It is the same procedure used for catching crayfish with a can, and at times it can also be used on blacks in the shallows after dark.

Keeping madtoms is little trouble for the do-it-yourself baitman because of the relative toughness of this bait. Any container from washtubs to horse tanks or aquariums will do nicely. Oxygenation is as much a must as with other baitfish, and the horned critters will eat just about anything from grubs and worms to nymph larvae.

Bee Moth Larvae

Bee moths' larvae, or waxworms to most fishermen, are one of the most sought after live baits, especially where panfish are concerned whether it be spring, summer, fall, or winter. In the wild, waxworms are found in only one location, that of beehives. The adults, "bee or wax moth" lay their eggs on the hive where the juveniles, once hatched, burrow into the honey combs feeding on wax, stored pollen, and impurities found in the hive.

The best way for do-it-yourselfers to handle obtaining a ready supply of waxworms for their fishing needs is to raise their own. With a few for seed either from a bait dealer or from an actual beehive, this will not be at all hard. All one needs in the way of materials is a half dozen or so gallon jars, some wax paper, and one of the many formulas for providing a medium for the raising of the young larvae to size. One such mixture is as follows:

12 ounces cereal (prepared or flakes)

2 ounces brewers yeast (powdered)

3 ounces each of bees wax and water

6 ounces of glycerin

7 ounces of honey

Shave the wax into small pieces and mix with yeast and cereal. In separate container mix the liquid components thoroughly then slowly add to the dry components. Make sure the mixture is moist but not sticky. Transfer the mixture to a jar, filling it about half way, and do not pack down. Cut the wax paper into approximately four inch squares, then fold up accordion style, stapling in the middle so fold can be spread slightly and place it in the jar also. Finally, add breeders and cover the jar opening with fine screen or cloth held in place with a rubber band or string. Set the jar in a warm, dark place (or cover with a dark cloth) and set aside. In about a week or so the adults will hatch and lay eggs in the wax paper, which can be left in that jar or moved to another. Kept warm enough, you should have worms for fishing in about thirty days or

Figure 20. Bee Moths or Waxworms can be raised by formulas, then stored in the refrigerator for at least a couple of months.

less, and the leftovers can be stored for further use. When that time comes, gather up some fine wood shavings from a local saw mill and place it and the waxworms in a reclaimed cottage cheese container. Placed in the refrigerator, they should hold up for at least a couple of months, unless of course the fish clean them out first. Either way, the results will be satisfying.

Sandworms

In the adult form, that is to say a Cranefly, sandworms have the look of a giant mosquito. They are related, but the craneflies lack the necessary tools and bloodthirsty nature of those nemeses of outdoor folk. In the juvenile stage, which is what live bait anglers are most interested in, craneflies look a lot like a grey accordion in a grub body.

There are roughly 300 species of cranefly living in the U.S., some coming from the soil and some from water. The aquatic varieties will do anglers the most good, and they can be found in habitat such as sunken leaf and debris piles along rivers and streams where current is lax. Their life as a larvae only lasts a few weeks before they pupate, so they must be gathered at once as soon as they are located.

The easiest way to harvest is with a net or converted shovel, sifting the gathered material on the bank in order to separate the worms. In order to stop the development process, they will have to be cooled as soon as possible. As for material, or bedding as it were, the same leaves, bits of wood and other assorted refuse from the stream will do fine. As for appeal, they will do in everything from bluegills to smallmouth bass and trout without an iota of discrimination.

Goldenrod Grubs

Finally, there is one other bait that falls into the miscellaneous category, which is the Goldenrod Grub. These grubs are a big hit with winter fishermen due to the damage they are known to do to bluegills. Winter also happens to be just about the only time they can be used due to their life cycle.

Goldenrod grubs are actually part of a large family of gall worms sired by wasp like flies called Cynipids. Other relatives can

Figure 21. Golden Rod Grubs are part of a large family of gall worms sired by wasp flies called Cynipids.

be found in the swelled tissue of plants (galls) such as oak, apples, and rose or blackberry. These plants characteristically swell up in the fall after the egg has hatched in the worm stage, whereupon the immature insects spend the winter feeding on the plant and its juices until a spring hatch.

Collection is easy, with the post frost plant stem being cut above and below the swollen portion, and then the stems are stored in a cool place such as basement or garage until used.

Chapter 8

Dead Bait Too

Since this bound batch of words is indeed titled, *"The Complete Bait Angler's Guide"*, something ought to be mentioned in regards to fish catching morsels that, to say the least, are no longer among the living. Naturally, there are some fisherfolk who — being purists in their own right — are apt to shun the thought in favor of something that wiggles of its own accord. But! Dead bait can catch fish too, which it quite often must when circumstances make the live stuff unavailable, taboo, or just plain unhandy.

It may help to consider dead bait in another light. Stop and ponder for a moment the minnow impaled on a jig hook by way of jaw through skull, or a wadded worm on a hook. Both examples are about as close to kicking the proverbial bucket as you can get.

A case that precludes live bait altogether might be a long backpack trip to some secluded trout lake in the mountains. Too, there are laws on the books of many states — countries also — that prohibit the transport of live non-native species across lines of boundary. Such instances make dead bait the only way to go, if one plans on putting meat to good use that is.

Today, live bait now preserved is readily available in many up-to-date tackle shops in familiar forms such as shiner and fathead minnows, smelt, crayfish, alewives, crickets, crawlers, waxworms, and leeches. Generally, these are either pickled so to speak, in a liquid form that has a base formed primarily of formaldehyde, or freeze dried. Of the two, freeze drying is preferred under most circumstances since formaldehyde carries a definite odor that may prove offensive to most fish. Dried bait may also be more compatible when backpacking and the like because of weight consideration also.

When time to fish, freeze dried bait requires that water be added to those deceased offerings for the space of a half hour or so before they fill out to former form, and thickness. The preparation does not hold up as long as formaldehyde, and those baits that have been opened should be used up within at least a day or two if possible. Decompostion will usually set in rapidly if any more time elapses.

Do-it-yourself bait chasers are not left to rummage about in tackle stores looking for what they need by any means. In the case of baitfish such as chubs, suckers, and shiners (which are the only ones commercially available anyway), simply freezing them in water until the fishing day arrives will do the trick. They can also be put into freezer bags — minus the H_2O — and be usable as a sort-of homemade freeze dry product. In either case, unless you want some weird, crooked forms once thawed, crack them at the base of the skull before processing.

Another baitfish, smelt, does a better job of catching fish when they are dead. Collecting them is best done in the spring during their spawning runs up tributaries. Tasty though they are, keep some for bait during summer or winter by treating them the same way as the other baitfish just mentioned.

Both crickets and grasshoppers can be placed in plastic bags and frozen for later use. Ditto with waxworms and wasp larvae, along with spikes, although all must be used quickly once thawed because they turn soft, especially under warm weather conditions.

Another prime candidate for home preservation are crayfish, which gives anglers the same two options as with baitfish, bagging or layered in milk cartons and frozen in water.

Rigging and Fishing

Fishing dead baits requires that anglers pick and choose their presentations and hook setups carefully. While, in most cases, the need is to rig for maximum action lacking the more natural enticement of a breathing bait's kicks and wiggles, anglers must guard against hook placements that are easily torn loose on the cast or retrieve.

Many times, the best way to make use of dead baitfish is with a jig, and an added stinger hook, especially when fishing cold water. The main hook can be run up through the skull, while the short stinger — utilizing a small treble hook — is placed somewhere beyond the anal fin of the baitfish.

Weight-forward spinners, such as the Erie Dearie so popular on Lake Erie these days, are another option, as are June Bug Spinners and their close resemblances. All of these more or less straight shaft spinners provide the flash appeal that mimics the real thing, often lacking in dead baitfish after handling.

For big pike, large odiferous baitfish such as smelt and cisco can be fished close to or right on the bottom with no action what-so-

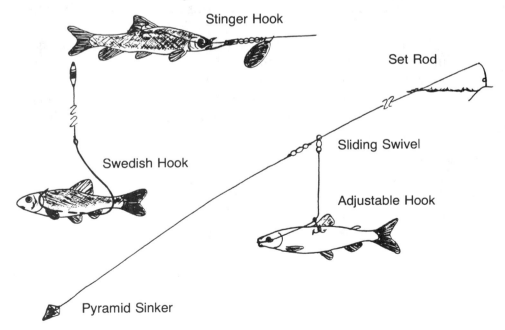

Figure 22. Dead Bait Riggings

ever, owing to the fact that oversized pike are scavengers to a large degree. Increasingly popular in North America, such setups have been a basic part of pike fishing in Europe for years. Various hook arrangements are used, but all are placed so that the waterwolves can be struck quickly, and held, once a bait is picked up.

Resurrected crayfish lend themselves to set fishing too, especially when the targets are the likes of catfish. Trout and bass fall for them when drifted in rivers and streams. For lake fishing, a lead head and a hop or lift/drop bringback will stir up action from a wide array of fish, depending on the size of the crawdad.

Light wire hooks are a must for crickets, grasshoppers, and soft baits such as waxworms. All should be completely impaled from tip to stern or vice versa due to their soft condition, thus avoiding the greatest share of throw offs and nibble offs.

As for leeches, tough as ever might be an apt description. Pick a way to present them and more than likely it will work, from weight-forward spinners to leadheaded jigs. Crawlers are far less durable, softening quickly and tearing easily, so it is best to put them to work where they can be hooked more than once and not lose any appeal. Set fishing and drift fishing are two options along this line.

More than likely, there are other ways — and other baits — in the field of preserved fish catching morsels that will do as well as those mentioned. One thing all must conform to however is the fact that they are indeed, "dead bait". As such it is up to the angler to figure out how, when, and where they are best put to use.

Chapter 9

The Business End

Even though many might not give it a thought, to the live bait fisherman, choosing the hooks he or she will use is as important to overall success as when and where the angling is or what the fishing is done with. It will not be the easiest of decisions, compounded by the number of choices touted and marketed by hook manufacturers. Then too, there are the inevitable tales from other angler types that entail the likes of musky caught on salmon egg hooks and the sight of a stringer of jumbo gills in the hands of a lad using hooks more in tune with sturgeon fishing. Such mental encumbrances tend to sway one's reason just a tad when you are in a tackle store.

Selecting the bent steel that gets attached to the line and stuck into the live bait is as much a matter of common sense as angling sense I suppose. Clinches such as "Big hooks for big bait and big fish," for example, do not always render the truth of the matter. Rather, wise bait fishermen keep a variety of styles and sizes in their tackle boxes to meet the needs of fishing day to day, bait to bait, and lake to lake; always bearing in mind that the word "natural" be uppermost. After all, that is what live bait fishing — if indeed effective — is all about, making a raw morsel appear as realistic as possible.

Hook Types

Perhaps one of the best all around types, or styles, of hook for the live bait angler is the salmon egg — with upturned eye — due to its compact easily concealable size, and all around hooking capabilities. Too often thought of as a trout angler's tool, they can handle baits for bluegills and pike ranging in sizes from a #10 up to a 2/0 for large minnows. The smaller versions in bronze virtually disappear in the nose of a leech or crawlers, which makes them ideal for slip sinker rigs and deep water trolling for the likes of walleyes, smallmouth, and trout.

Egg hooks also find another ready application when it comes to drift fishing rivers and streams, whether it be for rainbows or catfish. With that compactness and wide bend, egg hooks fit neatly under the collars of nymphs such as wigglers and stoneflies, through the tails of a crawdad, and even in larger sizes for other bait marriages and are still lightweight enough to allow current to carry them along quite naturally in all but the slowest streams.

As good as the salmon egg hooks are, the most widely used and familiar hooks are the aberdeens. Characterized by their light wire and slightly squared round bend construction much like a European "Model Perfect" hook, aberdeens are available in sizes from #12 to a 5/0. They also come in an extra long shank style or model that some crappie anglers in the south, and northern cricket fishers would not be caught without.

Given the fact that they are tempered to allow anglers the option of straightening them out before breaking lines, these hooks are ideal for novice and veteran alike when it comes to fishing snag filled waters. Still, they will hook — and hold with proper technique — everything from perch to big pike, and are especially suited for use with minnows, crawlers, and leeches when they are lip or nose hooked. They are noted for keeping bait healthy on a hook longer due to less than excessive puncture holes made on insertion.

A threesome of hooks closely related to the salmon egg styles, and more than adequate for many of the needs of the modern

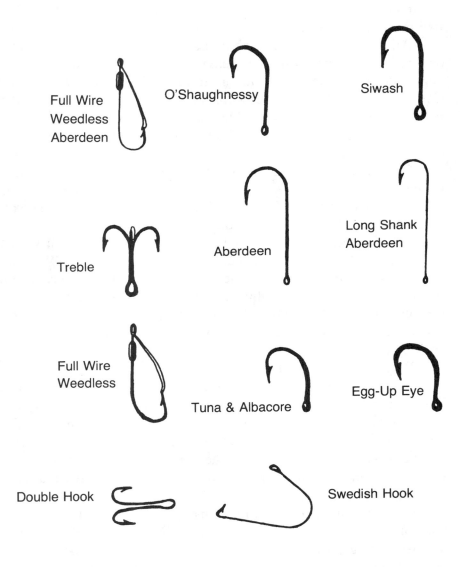

Figure 23. Hook Types and Styles

baitfisherman, are the Tuna & Albacore - Octopus - Siwash models. All three hooks meet the requirements where big, powerful fish like musky, salmon, steelhead, catfish, and pike are sought.

All three hooks are available in sizes that run from #8 up to ocean going models, and exhibit heavy, extra-strong wire that allows anglers to muscle fish when the need arises. Both the Siwash and Octopus styles offer a slightly longer shank and more extended point for deeper penetration and less throw offs where jumpers like steelhead are concerned. Of the three, the Octopus is the only "up eye" in the group.

Since bait tossers are almost sure to find themselves fishing greenery such as cabbage, reeds, coontail, and even milfoil on occasion, there is a definite need for some type of weedless hook in the arsenal. Fitting the bill in that respect are the weedless plain shanked and aberdeen hooks made by Eagle Claw, with full wire weedguard, which slips under the hook point itself. The 249W and 449W (baitholder barbed) are the better choices in the pads with frogs, sallies, and such, while the aberdeen 349W is great for leeches and other light baits. In both cases, anglers will find their performance well above split wire or other types of weedguarded hooks.

Where live bait fishing is concerned, there is a real need for various sized treble hooks as part of tackle box paraphernalia also. Trebles can be put to use in many ways, such as stinger hooks on jigs, as main hooks for flipping crawlers and crabs in stump or pad fields, and in specific cases, for use with minnows. There are other instances as well. Anglers need them for dead bait fishing, set fishing in rivers at times, and for trolling under some presentation requirements.

Of course, there are other modern day replacements for ancient bone and safety pins that fishermen may find of some use in their live bait fishing quests. With at least three major hook manufacturers plying the tackle market, freedom of choice is assured.

Jigs
One can consider jigs as just another offshoot of the world of fishing hooks, not a separate entity, especially since they have been

on fishing lines at least as long, historically speaking. Too often in today's angling, jigs go begging for use with live bait add ons, yet they fit into meat fishing like a good glove.

Like crankbaits who exhibit virtually the same body style yet work deep or shallow depending on the plastic lip, jigs offer much the same options. They are certainly far more than lead, hair, and hook. In modern tackle shops, anglers will quickly see that they have a wide choice when it comes to sizes, head styles, body material, and colors.

The four basic head designs of today's leadheads are ball, keel, fulcrum, and standup. Ball jigs look, as the name implies, like a round sphere with hook eye at the top. Keel jigs are wedge

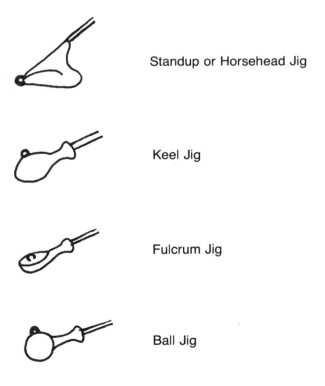

Standup or Horsehead Jig

Keel Jig

Fulcrum Jig

Ball Jig

Figure 24. Basic Jig Head Styles

shaped with tapered noses and flat sides that allow the head to ride vertically in the water under flow conditions. Again, hook eyes are at the top. Fulcrum jigs are distinguished by their more or less flat bodies that lie horizontal in or out of the water, and eyes can be found either at the top of the head or near the nose. Standup leadheads are almost a cross between keels and fulcrums, designed to let the hook stand up as the jig rests on the bottom. With their flat belly and basically pyramid or wedged back, they do this rather well. On these jigs, hook eyes are mostly at the top, but they can also be found near the nose at times.

Learning leadhead designs is paramount to success, whether they be fished solo or with the various live baits. Each type can usually be found to fit a particular situation better than the others. For example, ball jigs work well in lake fishing from shallow unobstructed waters to moderate depth levels down to perhaps 20-25 feet. Other than slow flow areas, they do not do as well in rivers where current causes them to roll quite a bit.

Wedge shaped keel jigs, on the other hand, cut current very easily, and are as good when an angler needs to get his bait deep quickly in some lake or reservoir fishing. Fulcrums offer more resistance in the water with their flat belly, therefore sinking slower, which means they are a better pick for slow retrieves, gently sloping bottoms conditions, or suspended fish. The standup jigs are the ultimate slow down lure, since they can literally be left sitting on the bottom while the likes of a live leech, crawler or minnow struggles in the readily visible to fish position resulting from an upright hook.

Live baiters who wish to add lead to their bag of tricks need not worry as to which bait might go with certain jigs, but rather select the live morsel in regards to their quarry. From tipping jigs with a waxworm for bluegills and perch to adding a six inch water-dog for bass, pike, or musky, any breathing bait will produce on any jig type. More important, is to learn which type of body material appeals to individual fish in certain bodies of water and at particular times of the year.

Most modern jigs run the gauntlet from the plain naked lead and hook head to fat full bodies rubber leg material called "living rubber", tied backwards to puff out. In between, live bait and jig anglers will find marabou, deer hair, feathers, tinsel, and plastic bodies such as grubs, minnows, or short worms. Then too, there are the inevitable myriad of colors, patterns, and combinations of material to consider.

Generally speaking, the more sought after fish species exhibit preferences tied to the time of year and the subsequent metabolic changes in their systems that tells them they need to eat more or less, bigger or smaller forage. A three pound largemouth is likely to make short work of a full bodied rubber leg jig and accompanying six inch leech in the fall as it tries to store up body fat for the coming winter. Depending on conditions, this same fish will be more inclined to choose a less bulky three inch grub and jig tipped with a crappie minnow, say, six weeks further on in the year with by then much cooler waters.

The basic habits of each species should also be of prime importance to jig and baiters. Some fish just do not like large offerings on the whole. Smallmouth bass and crappie are two good examples, both of which seem to opt for smaller offerings as they progress further in their adult lives. Pike and musky like mouthfuls at any age, and just about any time of the year, with only their ability to acquire such food stuffs in as leisurely a manner as possible a more critical factor.

Selecting body materials where jigs and live bait are concerned plays a vital role in whether or not the marriage will fit the situation an angler is faced with. The bottom line is that body material affects how a leadhead acts or reacts in the water. The choice can be especially critical in off activity periods such as late fall/early winter, early spring, or during those post cold front conditions so common to summer angling; not to mention where specific species are concerned. By and large, bodies figure to do or need the following once under the surface.

Fat or non-tailed grubs, stiff nylon and deer hair are least active on their own, needing retrieves that incorporate active jerks or twitches to make them appear alive. More pliable hair, such as marabou and thin swimming tailed grubs like minnow imitations, activate easily with just about any movement in the moderate range.

Rubber legged leadheads will quiver at the slightest touch, even a
bump of the rod if the line is tight at the time. Given these characteristics, a deer hair body might not be all that great a choice for
a late fall largemouth, no matter what the bait add on, especially
if that fish wants movement but not the violence of a belly dancer
registering on the Richter Scale. More appropriate would probably
be living rubber for the bass. On the other hand, a hungry northern,
who is quite active in cold water, is likely to pop the hair as soon
as he figures he has the angle.

Where lead jigs are involved, anglers can also make decisions
concerning hook sizes and styles just as they do with more standard
stickers. The ones most likely to show up on bait shop shelves are
the light wire aberdeens and the heavier o'shaughnessys. That being
the case, it is then a matter of picking out a size that fits the bait
and the fish. Light wires are available in sizes from #12 to a 4/0,
while the heavier o'shaughnessy can be had from a #8 to a 7/0.

Sometimes difficulty in using live bait on jigs comes in the
way of acquiring just what you want in a particular head style with
the right hook size or type. For those industrious enough to tackle
the task, the solution to such enigmas comes in the form of doing-it-
yourself manufacture wise, which is relatively simple these days.

Modern science and industry has come up with a silicone RTV
rubber mold making compound available through various lure component catalogs put out strictly for the amateur home manufacturer.
One such mail order house is Limit Manufacturing Company, Box
369, Richardson, Texas 75080.

The material, which usually comes in pound container sizes,
is combined with a hardening agent catalyst, and the entire mixture
placed in a paper or styrofoam cup. The chosen head design or
master jig is then placed in the cup also, suspended from pencil,
nail, or whatever and left for at least 24 hours so the compound
can harden. Once cured, the cup and material is split so that the
master can be removed. A sprue or pour hole is then cut into each
side at corresponding points.

What the angler is left with is a handy, usable leadhead jig
mold that allows him to pour exact duplicates of the intended jig.
After that, it is a simple matter of choosing hook sizes and styles

to fit the need. With economical clay like that found in hobby shops for use by school kids, anglers can also design their own heads. Once the hook is placed in the clay, the same procedure is followed for finishing the mold, and the results limited only by the fisherman's ingenuity.

Chapter 10

Equipment for Proper & Prolific Presentations

If they look around a bit, bait fishers will get plenty of chances to see renditions of their "fishing style". Scenes of lazy days, quiet bank or a small wood boat worthy of three men in a tub, with of course man's best friend in a snooze as though dead to the world. With the inevitable addition of the weatherbeaten old canepole and a float, the picture is complete. Classic Rockwellian calendar art that should warm the heart of anyone still breathing, but it does not do a whole lot as image goes for practicing live bait anglers these days. No wonder those who go au naturale have to put up with labels like "minnow bathers", "cricket dunkers", or "worm drowners".

Not so!, especially in today's world of space age tackle. Those making use of live bait morsels can work with the likes of fighting drags, computerized reels, and even fly rods just like the purists if they take a mind to. Even the classic canepole has gone state of the art with hollow-sectional fiberglass tubes capable of telescoping to twenty feet plus, which are ideal for transport in the baby cars found in most garages today. With all this, and much more, bait fishermen can cast, troll, fish top-bottom or inbetween as efficiently and effectively as anyone in their quest for filets.

Fiberglass Poles

If for no other reason than respect for things gone by, the stand-ins that replaced the bread and butter of live baiters for many years, fiberglass poles should be first when discussing current bait fishing equipment.

Progress never stays in place. Modern fiberglass poles are even lighter than relatives of ten years or so back, and in some cases, smaller in diameter as well. One thing has not changed though, and that is the trait of being perhaps the simplest fishing system short of a tree branch and bent pin.

Manufacturers like Lew's, B&M, plus others provide a choice of lengths for bait anglers from eleven to twenty-two feet, fully extended. Other characteristics, which number a grand total of two, are a tip eye and butt caps on each end when the rod is collapsed. A recent version also includes a package of slip on eyes, sizes and ringed for moving to the appropriate section of the pole.

Although glass poles are considered crude by a great many of the fishing persuasion due on part to their supposed limited line capacity, they have their place under certain circumstances. One of those involves angling for suspended panfish, and the line length need not be as limited as most think.

The solution to that problem is employment of either a small spinning or spincast reel taped to the rod near the angler end, (you can also substitute a fly reel spooled with mono rather than floating or sinking fly line). Given the option of a hundred plus yards of line with any of these reels and a slip bobber, suspended fish can be hunted at any depth. Also, with either the spin or spincast reels, glass poles can be used to cast, although grace would not be the word to describe such efforts, which are more of a sidearm lob than anything else.

For more conventional, meaning shallower, use of long poles, line is held by what are simply called "line keepers", being light metal strips with "L" shaped arms that extend inverted so the line can be wound around them. To hold them in place on the poles, a wrap around spring clips to the holder. Set up this way, fiberglass poles are an excellent tool for what is known by a couple of dozen local handles, actually amounting to short line vertical fishing in the shallows. Call it dabbling, dipping, flipping or whatever, for bass, pickerel, crappies, gills, and catfish in and around stumps, lily pads, or timber, it entails little more than dropping live bait close to these structures, with or without a bobber to signal a taker.

Spinning And Spincast Reels

Generally, spinning reels see the greatest use today among dedicated live bait types, being well aware of their capabilities with light lines and light weight sinkers, ideal for live bait fishing needs. The spinning reel's greater longevity of use without malfunction over brethren spincast reels and less need for the expertise of casting mechanics compared with baitcast (free-spool) reels are two other factors in that concensus also.

The first spinning reels came by way of several innovative anglers, all of whom were native to Europe. The first patent on the reel type itself was issued to one Alfred Holden Illingworth, and the first glimpses of the revolutionary new reels came to the American public in 1935. However, they were not to be allowed to put them to work until much later. The imports of the reel were held up by the conflagration that was to engulf almost the entire world before its ending, and they did not see the U.S. market again until 1947.

The uniqueness of the spinning reel's popularity and broad use comes from a fixed spool that allows the line to flow or uncoil through the weight at the line's end without the need to overcome inertia like that created when working with a revolving spool such as those found on baitcast reels. Since that fixed spool does not offer any initial resistance, it also practically eliminates the professional override (backlash), which crops up from time to time even in the best fishermen's efforts.

With spinning reels, anglers get a choice of three sizes, from small ultra-lights to ocean size, differentiated also by their gear ratios and line capacities. Virtually all can be made to fit the bill of the live bait fisherman by way of his particular angling situation or comfort with a certain size, make, or model.

Spincast reels are sort of a cross between conventional baitcast types and true spinning. A mongrel if you will, incorporating the use of the angler's thumb on a push button at the rear of the reel usually as though a free-spool, while the line peels off a fixed spool like the true spinning types.

The use of spincast reels is generally more suited to the heavier line weights and specific aspects of live baiting such as short cast bobber fishing or set fishing where a heavier sinker is employed due to a couple of trouble spots. The first of those involves friction build up which is found where the line leaves the enclosed (capped) spool through a narrow hole, cutting distance to the maximum with smaller weights. The other potential re-occuring problem is the likelihood of unseen loops along the spool as the line is retrieved, especially with thin diameter lighter monofilament. One other quirk that can affect the usefulness of those reels, specifically where bait anglers are involved, is the lack of feel due to minimal or non-existent contact with the line.

Baitcasting Or Free-Spool Reels

Baitcasting, or in more modern verbiage, free-spool reels have a long, rich history, due no doubt to the birth in the most primitive stages as the "Kentucky Reel". In 1810, the first true multiplying reel came to light under the hand of George Snyder, a Kentucky watchmaker.

In those early days, those premier reels were specifically designed for live baiters who fished with minnows. The approved method was to coil the line-fine silk usually raw — in hand or on the bottom of the boat and with the aid of a native wood rod like hickory or osage, swing the bait outward, letting the force of the rod and bait uncoil the line. What Mr. Snyder did was to build a more delicate spool that cut down inertia, with gearing that revolved the spool several times with each turn of the reel handle.

Such was the state of baitcasting reels until the 1880's when Benjamin Meeks re-entered the reel making business after a hiatus of some thirty-five years, having been a partner previous to that period with both his brother Jonathon and Ben Milam. Although both men were famous reel designers in their own right, Meeks brought back with him a revolutionary change to spiral gearing that replaced then standard spur gears, the introduction of jewel pivot bearings that reduced wear, and most important of all, manufacturing as an organized process. In other words, mass production in an early form that elevated baitcasting to true popularity. These changes also made it possible to use shorter rods with the likes of the recently invented "Dowagiac Minnow", in conjunction with "Kalamazoo" cast, not to be confused with the Kazoo cast where the angler lets fly and the lure zooms into the water at one's feet.

One final chapter in the free-spool's development, perhaps the most significant, came through a Wisconsin firm, Wheeler & McGregor, who invented a level wind mechanism. That made things easier for fisherfolk, laying line back on the reel evenly and distributing it the same during the cast almost eliminating the backlash entirely, except for those human lapses we all are plagued with on occasion, even today.

The place for free-spool reels in the repertoire of modern bait fishermen, like the spincast reel, is a varied one. For situations such as trolling, bobber fishing larger baits such as minnows, and casting certain jigs-n-bait marriages, they fit in extremely well, especially with modern state of the art reels. Being the heavy duty component of the entire reel spectrum, they also are a must where bait tossers expect to come across the likes of musky, large pike, giant catfish, or the salmonoids.

Fly Reels

The final member of the quadruple group of angling tools designed to hold the connection — namely line — between fish and man is the fly reel. Being the eldest of the line holders, before their advent, it was up to the angler and long wippy rod to hold the fish at bay until landing.

Modern fly reels come in two forms, single action, which means the angler is the means of retrieval by cranking the line in himself, and automatic reels that retrieve line with the touch of a lever near the reel bottom. They come in a wide range of sizes for panfish up to ocean angling. In any case, fly reels are designed basically for storage purposes, not fish playing tools, which should always be kept in mind.

Where live bait fishermen are concerned, fly reels should always be coupled with the intended rod for practical and successful fishing. The entire outfit will find its most appropriate niche in spring and fall's shallow water fisheries for panfish in lakes and reservoirs. Warm weather workings with the long rods are more limited to streams and rivers where they can be fished with both floatable and submersible insects such as crickets, grasshoppers, nymphs, and leeches. Underwater drifts in such waters for trout, catfish, and smallmouth can also include baitfish and crawdads if the angler is careful to adjust his or her casting style considerably so as not to fling these morsels into the stratosphere. More standard tactics with accepted insect artificials can also be productive for live bait types who will combine purist ethics with the likes of say, a waxworm, leafworm, or spike, which is unethical only if you take more than your limit.

Rods

In virtually every instance where a reel is employed, so too must the fishing rod. That sounds like a brilliant statement, akin to calling Pike's Peak a mountain, but a fishing rod is a long way from being a pole in this day and age where new materials have aged fiberglass to the point of extinction. For live bait fishermen, these new rods are just as important to their angling success as they are to the purists angler be they fly, crankbait, or plastic worm fishermen; users of fly, spinning or casting outfits.

The best rods, in this angler's opinion, are the graphites — pure graphites that is — not the composite rods made up of graphite and fiberglass composition. However, composites are not a complete out, especially since the cost of pure graphites may be beyond the means of many anglers. The trick to acquiring a good composite rod is to look closely at the content ratio between the two components. These are usually imprinted near the reel seat, along with recommended lure and line weights. If no such information is listed on the rod, find one where it is, and purchase that one with the highest graphite content.

Boron is another relatively new material reaching the outlets where fishermen gather small fortune's worth of equipment in order to pursue their sport. Being even more cost prohibitive than graphite, boron rod buyers should follow the same guidelines for purchase as if buying a graphite, being aware of content most of all.

The main advantage to replacing glass rods with either boron or graphite, or composites with adequate graphite content of at least 80%, is twofold. First of all is the relative stiffness and strength of either material, although boron is foremost. This translates to faster and easier hook setting, not to mention casting ease as these rods load up quicker to help propel a bait. Other than shallow water fishing with short lines, the stretch factor in most modern monofilaments can make or break a hook set. Too limp a rod only aggravates the situation by not removing that stretch until well into the setting motion, meaning the chances of no set, or a slight set are maximized as a fish quickly ejects the thing that does not feel quite right as it seemingly pulls back.

With the fast setting motion, due to their stiffness and construction, graphite and boron rods usually only need half the exertion on the part of an angler. The lowering of a rod tip to the water and subsequent violent hook set that leaves the fisherman arching backward, rod behind the ear to the point of both falling out of the boat may make great pictures, but it is far from necessary. Beyond that, it is often ridiculous and costly, since such antics account for the breakage of plenty of expensive graphite and boron each year. Naturally, this is laid on the manufacturer, which is not the case at all if the fisherman will take a little time and replace the half brick with brain matter to make a full load.

The most distinct advantage of using graphite rods for live bait anglers is in the amount of feel they possess. With the right sinker weight, fishing in better than thirty feet of water, bait anglers will readily be able to distinguish between small rocks and gravel, sand or clay, and other structure changes with these rods and a little experience. In the case of using a baitfish, panic on the minnow's part as it nears a predator is easily telegraphed to the rod hand. Such knowledge of prey trying to escape oblivion with all its might is well worth the expenditure for a rod any day.

Chapter 11

Paraphernalia and Other Important Etceteras

True fishermen are as much collectors as anything else, that is for sure. If an angler has success or sees success on a particular color-style of worm, crankbait, or whatever, chances are he will have at least two or three of the same in his tackle box as soon as the opportunity to do so presents itself. In that regard, call it the wanton gathering of tackle, live bait fisherfolk may just be the worst of the lot, acquiring hooks and sinkers by the hundreds or at least dozens, full size ranges and spectrums of jigs in multiple of two or better, and so on. True, necessity is often a matter of mind. It is not a matter of having any will power, but rather a lack of will not power. Nevertheless, woe to the live bait angler caught chasing suspended walleyes without floating jig heads or fishing muddy stream browns minus the aid of a small spinner blade. Of such paraphernalia limits are often made.

There is no easy way to describe adequately the filling of a tackle box - nor an organized one - when it comes to the various components needed for successful bait fishing. Murphy's Law, at least one of them, dictates that some items will be missed in any event, but never mind that. If you need it, or think you need it, put it in. You never know.

The Basics

Already covered have been hook styles that bait anglers find most useful, along with jigs. However, in order to make the connection between that main line and the pointed steel when fishing, the likes of slip sinker, drift, and some set fishing rigs, anglers find the need for snell making materials. Why not just purchase pre-tied commercial snells, thus saving both time and room in the tackle box? Frankly, they do not always do the job, being both too heavy line size wise and not long enough for all - indeed most - situations.

In order to be fully prepared for all contingencies, bait fisher boxes should be stocked with 2, 4, 6, 8, 10, and perhaps 12 lb. test spools in at least the sixty yard capacity size. This range will cover just about everything from perch to steelhead where snells are involved in the various presentations.

To go along with snells, in order to be able to attach them, comes swivels' both the barrel variety for the slip sinker rigs and three-ways for set and drift fishing. Swivel sizes, be they either type, should be on the small side, and black if possible in order to avoid detection by the fish under most circumstances. Size ten in the barrel swivel is generally acceptable, and in the three-way, size eight is sufficient for most situations.

When it comes to sinkers, bait tossers need a plethora of sizes and styles. Among the most useful are slip sinkers, of which there are three styles, foremost of them being the bottom walkers.

Bottom walkers are designed to be used while the bait is on the move as in trolling, back-trolling or drifting (from a boat as opposed to drift fishing while wading rivers and streams). These leads are elongated or upright with a line hole at the top so that the base barely touches or drags the bottom, yet keeps hang ups to a minimum. This is especially true over rock or boulder strewn stream bottoms and the like. The two most recognized names on the market these days are Lindy's and Crawford.

Worm sinkers are next in line for a berth in tackle box drawers, being most identified with the use of plastic worms, but ideal for

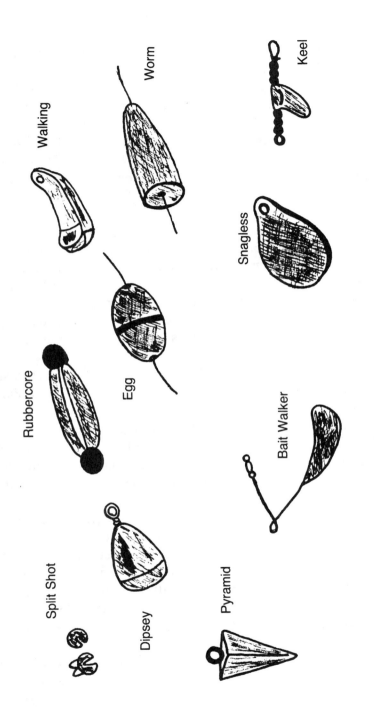

Split Shot

Dipsey

Pyramid

Rubbercore

Egg

Walking

Worm

Snagless

Bait Walker

Keel

Figure 24. Sinker Types

live bait approaches as well. These leads are designed to rest horizontally on the bottom, line hole running through from tapered nose to rounded rear end, which may be either flat or indented. They are very practical in lake weed beds for species from bluegills to northerns.

Another kind of sinker live bait anglers will find fitting for many of their outings is the egg sinker. As the name implies, these leads are egg shaped, with hole from end to end just like the worm sinkers. They are especially good choices for set fishing on the bottom in lake or river.

Finally, the last of the slip sinker styles are labeled slip shot, being exactly what the name describes, a piece of lead shot with line hole through the center. Slip shot come in handy for shallow or slack water fishing in either lake or stream, and with a little practice can be worked thru and over certain types of fish holding debris on the bottom such as rocks, timber, and light weeds. They are an excellent pick for smaller baits and very light line such as 2-4 lb. test.

Still more weights live bait fishermen can put to good use are the fixed sinkers, some for a wide scope of situations and some more specialized. By fixed, they are designed to be tied directly to the line in a set position like at the end of the line for a double hook set fishing rig, above the hook under a bobber or on a three-way swivel drift fishing rig. The most recognized among this batch are probably the bell sinkers, or dipsey sinkers as they are sometimes called.

Bells are shaped exactly like worm sinkers. In fact, a pair of needle nosed pliers and a few twists and bends to remove the pin that runs through the center will give anglers just that in a pinch, a slip sinker. Bells are used in both moving and nonflow water.

One fixed sinker designed specifically for set fishing in rivers carries the name snagless. These are flat, sort of wide tear drop shaped leads that avoid the effects of all but the heaviest current flows.

Another tie direct non-moveable lead designed for special work is the pyramid sinker. These are for use in soft bottoms, and big waters where current or undertow would tie other rigs in knots. Shaped just as the name implies, their pointed nose plunges into the bottom, hopefully holding the bait setup in one spot. Likely spots for their use are the Great Lakes and seacoast where surf fishing is likely.

Of course, virtually all anglers are aware of what a split shot is designed for and does. Shot are the mainstays of the sinker world, good for set fishing, casting weight, as well as critical to the use of floats from slip bobbers to the quill variety. They are of the fixed lead family, to be pinched on the line with the aid of pliers or perhaps a tooth, but the latter litter the bottom from Maine to Alaska due to the lack of other more appropriate equipment for attaching lead to a line.

Under the sinker realm, there are two other types that may come in handy for bait anglers from time to time, one definitely of the fixed kind, and one that while not being a slip sinker is regulated to one position on the line either.

The one position only sinker of this duo is the keel sinker, which is just like it sounds, a piece of lead with a keel or rutter to guide it through the water in an upright non-rolling position. Keel sinkers are made so that they must be tied to the main line with a snell running off the rear of the lead. On both ends of the sinker are a series of beads in a chain with eye on the main line side and clip on the bait end, making them ideal for what their primary purpose is, pure and simple trolling.

Rubbercore sinkers can best be described as oblong lead with a rubber insert that is twisted once the line is placed behind it, thus holding a fixed position, but moveable if one chooses. This characteristic makes rubbercores ideal for use in both rivers and lakes where suspended fish may need longer line lengths between weight and bait to float high enough to reach the fish. Tapered as they are, these sinkers can also be worked through some types of cover without too many hang ups if bait fishermen are careful.

The next step to a well stocked tackle box is to gather up a few bobbers for use where suspended fish are too high off the bottom or too far below the surface for effective fishing by other means. Bobbers are also handy for certain types of drift fishing with live bait for the likes of walleye and smallmouth, as well as catfish and steelhead.

Perhaps the most versatile and therefore practical type of floats are the slip bobbers, which make use of either braided line, plastic, or wire stops to control bait depth. With them, casting is a breeze since the stop can be brought right onto the reel spool itself and the bobber slips down the line to where the sinker is set. Clip on floats obviously have the drawback where depth ranges are greater than 6-8 feet because they must remain stationary on the line, thus making casting near impossible beyond that depth range setting.

Bobber size and shape, to all but the uninitiated, is critical since too much buoyancy tattletales to the fish that something is not quite right where his intended meal is concerned. If one gets a choice, short and thin is the way to go, with thin the priority. Generally speaking, floats with a diameter no larger than an inch to inch and a quarter do the best job.

Shallow water fishing that gets away with clip on bobbers finds a wide choice of makes for bait anglers if they choose not to go the slip bobber route. Among the most popular are the round plastic kind, where the line is attached on the bottom, wood types that are available in small-medium-large oval or pencil shapes also attached at the base, and plastic tapered spin floats that either allow the line to be run thru the middle's rubber twist lock or tied to a screw eye on one end, leader or snell on the other.

There is one other fixed depth bobber, ancient enough to have known Boone or Crockett. Originally, quill floats were just that, porcupine quills, preferably the already discarded ones. Modern versions are often plastic - what is not these days - but have the same qualities of thinness, and light weight that makes them highly undetectible by most fish, and therefore most useful in many shallow water bait fishing angles.

Attractors

One might think that live bait needs no help in getting the attention of fish. Normally it does not, but there are times when tantalizing wiggles and scent appeal need a little help. Think of it this way. In all likelihood, adding a pretty necklace or earrings helped push YOU over the edge once or twice. Most creatures are suckers for an extra bauble or two when even the slightest bit hesitant.

One thing that can make a difference in dark water, after dark, or in deep water is the addition of small blades, either Colorado - willow leaf - Indiana style. Placed on the line an inch above the hook, they add both attractive flash and vibration that aids fish in finding them and the bait, as well as enticing them to strike.

Knowing how each blade works helps. Colorado blades are known for moving a lot of water (noisier), and can be moved in a slow manner. Indiana blades, while more elongated and not as wide, work best at moderate speed or in current with like vibration. Willow leafs need speed to keep them moving, yet put out the least vibration.

Both size and color is of prime importance when one adds attractor blades. General rules dictate that in clear water smaller blades in subdued colors scare fewer fish. Stained or colored water and one goes the opposite direction, larger and brighter. While standard colors, as is from the punch press, are copper, bronze, chrome steel; modern technology has added the possibilities of the rainbow - in flourescent colors too - thanks to lure tape that can be cut to order. Hammered blades (dimpled) give off more flash than smooth ones, and lighter weight metal (thinner) vibrates harder than heavier blades, thus are more noisy. The softest sounding blades on the market today are the newer plastic types.

Naturally, there is a trick or two you might need from time to time. If colors are too flashy, carry a candle to smoke them up a bit by holding them over the flame which darkens them with a film. Try putting a dent in both Colorado and Indiana blades with the aid of a ballpeen hammer. Not too hard, and near the center will make a flat spot for more vibration, hence noise.

Of course, with blades, other tackle box "add ins" must include the clevices they will ride in and an assortment of beads to space them above the hook. Clevice sizes that will suffice are 1's and 2's, and as for bead sizes try 7/32, 3/16, and 5/32 inch sizes.

There are several other attractors that should find space in tackle boxes too, especially where bait fishers hope to add walleyes, bass, and trout to coolers. Floating jigs are one of these. Made from cork or hardened foam so that the lightweight hook rides inverted, they will be top picks for suspending a leech, nightcrawler, or minnow.

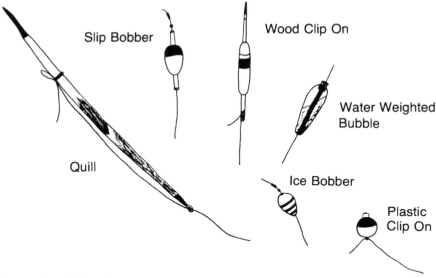

Figure 25. Bobber Styles

Suspension is also the byword of two more related, although primarily thought of as steelhead baits, namely wobble and spin-n-glos. However, they do a bang up job for gamefish other than the salmonoids in both lake and stream. With rubber wings, spin-n-glos are excellent for trolling or set fishing in moving water with either leeches or nightcrawlers. Wobble glos, which do just that - wobble from side to side, are capable trollers as well, and can be drift fished in either bass or trout stream as well. Both cork attractors are available in various sizes, but for most needs the medium sized bodies will do bait anglers the most good in a wide range of colors.

Extras
No bait fisherman's tackle box would be complete without a few added, but essential, extras. Finger nail clippers are great for snipping line, excess body material on jigs, and the like. One will also find need for scissors when cutting lure tape, and needle-nosed pliers for various and sundry duties.

Added insurance in order to keep minnows on a hook are plastic tait tabs punched out of pop can holders with a paper punch, and one more thing. Do not forget to stash a small needle and syringe or commercial air injector. That way, you can put a bubble of air into nightcrawlers, which not only makes them suspend as though natually drifting, but squirm more too.

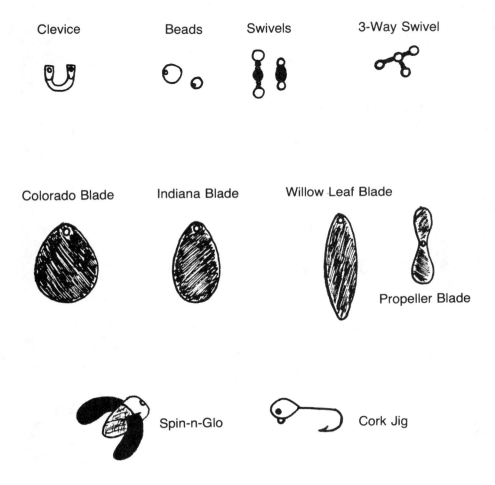

Figure 26. Live Bait Paraphernalia

Figure 28. Given though battles that put bass to shame, an amiable nature towards anglers, and tastiness, bluegill have a large following.

Chapter 12

Bluegill Means

One can describe the "King Of Panfishing" in a lot of ways, but perhaps the most appropriate is to say, "They are a fish of beginnings and endings." Many has been and will be the angler who cuts his fishing teeth on bluegills, gone on to other species, only to return to their pleasures once again as fishing years draw to a close.

Today, there are an estimated 15,000,000 or so dedicated bluegill fishermen plying their trade towards gathering a fish sack full of their beloved 'gills. Given those tough battles that put many a bass to shame, an amiable nature towards an angler's offerings, and tastiness on the platter that rivals the best beef or fowl, there ought to be more.

Thanks to their abilities as new stock for waters from farm ponds to impoundments, modern bluegill ranges have expanded, giving the opportunity for more folks to get in on the action. Originally, enclaves ran from Minnesota to the East Coast, south to Georgia, and west to Arkansas, but now they swim in virtually every section of the country.

Scientifically labeled *Lepomis machrochirus*, gills are a relative to both large and smallmouth bass, along with crappies, rock bass, and other sunfishes - yellowbreast, long ears, shellcrackers. All are members of the *Centrarchidae* or Sunfish Family, and although bluegills are known for being primarily a minimal or no flow fish, river anglers get suprised on a regular basis where dams or age have slowed down the water sufficiently.

To say the least, bluegills are prolific repopulators, which often leads to problems on smaller waters unless angling pressure helps supplement normal predation. Spawning temperatures for these feisty panfish average around 65-67 degrees, which means they may court as early as February or as late as August, depending on geographic location.

The males invade the shallows first during the spawn period, seeking nesting sites that allow them to fan out semi-round beds. The natural incubation chambers may be as shallow as a foot to as deep as twelve feet, all according to the clarity of a given body of H_2O, on bottoms of clay, sand, fine gravel, marl or some mixture of these elements.

When water temps reach the right point to complete metabolic changes, the she fish arrive from their pre-spawn locations off the first primary break to deposit as many as 30,000 plus eggs. Youngsters usually appear from three days to a week later, are guarded a short time by papa, then disperse. By the end of their third year in the northern areas of the country, they will have reached the neighborhood of six inches or so, if they survive, which many do not.

Spring Tactics

A great many bluegill chasers do not start their angling season in earnest until the word leaks out that fish are beginning to enter the shallows to set up housekeeping. Such delays are wasting plenty of fishing time, especially since earlier excursions inshore are a common bluegill characteristic. Gills do so simply because they are hungry.

Whether north or south, waters begin to warm - the shallowest ones first - as the sun returns from its winter position over the Southern Hemisphere, gradually tracking towards the top pole and summer. Doing so means increases in food chains made up of plankton, insects, small crustaceans, and bluegill activity, if one knows where to look.

Sun angles during this period place the greatest exposure on northern shorelines. Naturally, where Sol shines the brightest is where things begin to heat up first. Gill hunters can also figure that wind protected areas like bays, bayous, and channels in that direction also will benefit the greatest; calm water being non-reflective of the sun's rays. Reflection is also the key word in finding agreeable panfish as it relates to bottom types. Soft, dark bottoms like muck or mud absorb heat like a sponge while light shaded bottoms like clay, sand, and gravel take much longer to heat by comparison.

The earliest form of bluegilling in cool to cold water dictates that anglers keep their baits on the small side and presentations slow to correspond with bluegill metabolism. Such criteria makes grubs like mousies, waxworms, spikes, or wasp larvae better selections than full blown insects and worms. A large proportion of this type of spring bluegilling can often be done from bank or boot (waders) with the fish close enough inshore to cast to.

Plastic bubbles are one way to get the job done right in the shallow water when teamed up with the previously mentioned grubs, a single split shot, and small salmon egg hook. Even though bugs are not yet out of their overcoats, the likes of tiny versions of wet flies such as a black gnat, tipped with a bit of meat fished off the same rig works too. Fishing depths over four or five feet like those found in some channels or bays means a switch to slip bobber, but the basic retrieve which is no retrieve or just a slight twitch now and then are the same due to frigid fluid.

Eventually, waters will move out of the forties into the fifties as spring rolls along. Increased temperatures mean two things to the panfish, being even hungrier and more food to compensate, courtesy of Mom Nature. It also should tell anglers they can begin to expect activity in some main lake areas as more gill begin to stir.

During what amounts to early pre-spawn in main lake areas calls for some searching on the part of bluegill maniacs. In order to find the smaller scattered concentrations of cooperative fish normal to the time frame, movement is the key, magnified by the size of the body of water. Try trolling slowly with the aid of a quiet electric motor rather than a gas job in waters less than twenty feet deep. Drifting or oars may be as good or even better, especially if the lake is a clear one.

Back-trolling-movement in reverse, so as to utilize the control point at the stern for precise maneuvering - pays off in more fish in the twenty plus depth range. It also has the added effect of slowing progress down to a crawl if one kicks the engine in and out of gear, a must at times for slow feeders.

Regardless of which presentation lends itself to be the most productive, riggings and bait choices tend to follow certain guidelines. Those same grubs will still be fish getters, but bobber fishing them is pretty much out except for slow drifting or oaring. Not too many fish will be suspended high enough to warrant their use in the main lake areas during the period either. In the above twenty range, a slip shot so as to be able to adjust snell length as needed, is ideal. Bluegillers can also employ the wet fly gimmick with it also. A couple of standard shot, fixed eighteen to twenty inches above the bait will do as well, specifically when belly to the bottom bluegills are involved.

Deeper water requires more weight to go along with the change in approach needed for depth, namely a walking slip sinker, or worm type if preferred, that keeps the entire setup close to the boat for more control and feel of the lightest strike.

A wider choice is optional once waters get into the 50's, bait wise, as insect activity really gets going. Nymphs like wigglers, caddis and dragonfly larvae will all take bluegills now, as will small leaf worms and red worms.

As waters reach into the 60's, expect fast and furious fishing plain and simple. The slab-sided panfish will be gathering in numbers for the upcoming re-population rites nearest to their selective spawning sites. Look for them in spots with the previously described bottom content, and expect more attacks from males than females due to a tenfold increase in their belligerency button.

The long poles will do when the fish are on the beds, and are exceptionally effective when the gills are close to or among weed growth such as lily pads where anglers need to drop a bait rather than cast it. Once hooked, the panfish can be quickly hoisted from the cover without hanging up. Such close quarters also call for the use of those light wire aberdeens that can be straightened out with a steady pull then reformed for further use.

Bluegill spawning in the clearest of waters, although still aggressive, tends to require a stealthier approach, necessitating the use of spinning gear and casting to likely areas. This being the case, a good pair of polarized sunglasses aids in spotting bedding areas. Look for contrasts in the bottom such as light on dark or vice versa.

As obliging as bluegills are at this seasonal juncture, anglers have little worry as to what bait they will accept. More to the point, anything that even remotely resembles a threat to the eggs will be savagely attacked. Tiny crayfish with a shot pinched some six inches above the hook to keep them where the angler wants them, small minnows, and leeches all receive hot receptions. Tiny tube or swimming tail grubs in the inch size range tipped with a grub, or piece of worm get the same treatment.

Summer Period

Summer bluegill chasers should expect to do a bit of searching for their fish, perhaps even more than at any other time of the year. This aspect of panfish hunting has to do in great part to two factors, lake type and forage.

All lakes fall into three basic categories or classifications, with varying degrees of each, but bluegills are common to only two. Lakes with the highest fertility are shallower, darker due to algae growth, lack major breaklines into deep water, and have a variety of weed growth. Labeled eutrophic, they yield the greatest pounds of fish per acre, and are the oldest geologically speaking. Mid-age lakes are known as mesotrophic, characterized by clear to perhaps stained color, depths to go along with sharp drop offs, and weed growth made up of firm bottom flora such as cabbage, sandgrass, and some coontail.

In shallow lakes, bottoms are primarily made up of silt beyond the weedlines, a result of ageing. That in itself limits forage possibilities and the use of such areas other than suspension, but suspended fish are also vulnerable fish. The weedbeds in such waters grow in the firmest bottom, providing the majority of bluegills and other fish both a dining and living area that affords them cover as well.

On meso lakes, often times the situation is radically different with bottoms such as rock, gravel, clay and the like, allowing bluegills, especially the larger fish, to use deep water frequently at all depths, if not nearly all the time.

Fishing suspended bluegills with live bait successfully can be handled in several different ways during mid-summer. Drifting is one approach, aided by slip bobbers for depth control, until fish are located. At that point, most anglers will anchor and work the school, either by still fishing or casting and counting down their offering until they reach the gill's level, then slowly retrieving through the fish. Ideal baits for what are most likely neutral attitude fish (may bite-could bite) include crickets, hoppers, catalpa worms, leeches, and leaf or red worms. In all cases, the appearance of the bait, excepting leeches which by nature swim on their own, ought to be that of a morsel haplessly drifting along with the water flow. In other words, easy pickings to the panfish, sort of like a lone piece of candy sitting on your coffee table while you try to remain interested in that dull novel. Sooner or later you bite too.

Bluegills actively feeding is another matter. Fish attending a hatch may appear to feed in one spot, often tattletailing their presence by surface activity. During mid-summer, gills often run tiny bait fish too, boiling the water for a moment or two as the baitfish try to flee on the surface. Still fishing will get some fish for sure, but far more will come from aggressive casting to match the mood of the bluegills. Those small jigs with the tube or curly tails tipped with grubs, small leeches, and nymphs like wigglers get the most attention. Often times, they will be smacked as soon as they land. Riotous fishing indeed, but alas, not the norm.

Bluegilling for those fish out of sight is by far the most prevalent condition during the middle of the year, particularly in clear waters with deep weedlines, sunken islands, and rock humps. Such locales are favorites of the elders of the bluegill tribe.

Probing the depths is best handled with one of the slip sinker and bait rigs while on the move until fish are located. At that point, slip a marker buoy over the side to mark the spot for a return trip through the area, or back off and cast with one of those fly to bait rod conversions made for light line and almost weightless fishing with bait.

The old neutral attitude bugaboo can show up in deep water as well as elsewhere, but the likewise ancient enticement through easy eating can work down below too, with a little adaptation.

Utilizing either a sliding shot, egg or worm sinker in conjunction with a suspended bait is the answer to the problem. Suspension is handled with the aid of a tiny ice fishing bobber, floating jig provided the hook is small enough, or a styrofoam bead designed specifically for this means of presentation. With a very light wire aberdeen hook such as a #10, keeping the bait floating will be no problem.

The long rod allows you to throw two pound test with ease, which is ideal since it sinks rapidly due to its small diameter. this also means that light weight sinkers can be employed, and that the shock of a big bluegill on the light line will be absorbed by the rod, avoiding break-offs.

The mechanics are unfettered, simply a cast that lets the bait settle, then slowly retrieve, dragging the sinker ever so slightly with pauses in between. A pick up, quick two count, and Mr. Gill is on his way to the fish sack, then it's back for another. As for baits, try wigglers, small crayfish, tiny minnows, and leaf worm or crickets.

Autumn Angles

The early part of the fall season is handled much the same as summer fishing, with bluegills using the same haunts until the turnover which equalizes oxygen and temperature top to bottom, in preparation for the cooldown to ice up.

Beyond the turnover, things shift more towards deep water where all age groups of bluegills are concerned. As the waters cool, food chains shrink, and so does the panfish's metabolic rates. Large baits will not do the trick so a switch to grubs and nymphs are likely alternatives.

Likewise, presentations must slow down also. Still fishing

vertically with a tandem hook setup, complete with bell sinker at the bottom, is the best rigging. Many anglers go to ice rods over the side of the boat also, with the same tiny ice spoons used by hardwater anglers as attractors.

Ice Time

Upon ice up, the warmest water will be at the bottom of most lakes, but first ice does not mean the fish will be there just yet. One habit bluegill chasers can usually count on during the winter period is that these panfish will make one last foray into the shallows just after the waters coat over. It may last a couple of days, or perhaps a week or so, but action is usally fast for a time, although tactics are no different from those the rest of the winter.

The mainstay of a winter bluegill's dining menu is basically made up of one primary food source, and what amounts to a long shot second. Zooplankton are just about the only remnant of the food chain left, so bluegills have little choice of what to eat, and when is also up for grabs. These tiny animals have a habit, as mentioned previously, of rising and falling over the course of a day depending on light conditions. In order to take fish, winter anglers must plan on suspended fishing, so bobbers are a must, and they should be small ones to compensate for the light bites common to winter bluegilling.

Trying to adequately imitate microscopic plankton can be a chore. Using mousies, spikes, and waxworms on tiny ice spoons sporting #10 and 12 hooks comes the closest to the task. Also good at times are corn borers, wasp larvae, and goldenrod grubs. Given a lake with a fair population of nymph life during the warmer months, winter fishing can be good with wigglers, stonefly, and other aquatic larvae.

The only other bait that may take some fish during ice time, are tiny minnows in the inch long size range, but these will usually be shunned by the smaller gills.

In the case of either food source, fish move about quite a bit during winter, but it is usually in the context of relating to many of the same general areas of summer, only in the deepest water provided in that area.

Chapter 13

Perch Patterns

Tasty is a good word to describe the Yellow Perch. Gregarious, another. Put them together, along with gluttonous, and the combination is reason enough to go fishing. Millions do, some to the exclusion of all other species, where *Perca flavescens* is concerned.

Yellow perch are primarily a fish of cool, deep waters, namely lakes and reservoirs, but can and do inhabit smaller, shallower waters and some rivers. For quality fishing however it is the young and middle aged, hard bottomed and minimal weed growth lakes like Erie in Ohio and Mendota in Wisconsin that perch jerkers should concentrate on. Fortunately, with the exception of the southernmost parts of the nation, waters that meet the needs of these tasty panfish are widespread enough to provide plenty of perching.

The biological clock in these barred cousins of the walleye dictates that they spawn early in the spring, thus providing a steady forage base for their larger aquatic neighbors. Shortly after the pike lay eggs, followed by the walleyes, perch do their thing as water temperatures reach the upper forties. As per the norm, males visit the nesting sites, which are generally weedy shallows, first and leave last. On some waters with creeks or river outlets, perch will even migrate upstream to spawn.

The she fish lay around 50,000 eggs on the average in a jellylike mass strung over weeds, brush, or other bottom debris, which absorbs water to sustain the embryos. Fertilization is usually accomplished with the aid of several males moving side by side with the she fish as eggs are emitted. Both parents depart after the ritual, leaving eggs, which hatch in about 14 days, and the resulting fry on their own. Good conditions mean a 50% breakout rate for the youngsters, who school up and use cover as the primary means of escaping predator assaults. On the shallower lakes with heavy weeds, these tactics can be successful enough to result in overpopulation of the ringed panfish. That in turn leads to lots of 5-6 inchers on the hook, but little quality, hence the criteria that makes up a good perch lake mentioned earlier. When a stunted lake is come across by anglers, little can be done unless the DNR steps in, so it is better to just pack up and head for greener pastures.

Perch generally travel in schools made up of year class fish, uniform size, with grownups preferring deeper water most of the year. For the most part, these fish are daylight active so bright days do anglers the most good. Towards evening, or on dark days, they seem to settle belly to the bottom and remain pretty much inactive until things brighten up again.

Perch relish a wide list of live bait, naturally good news to the get-your-own bait tossing anglers. Topping the group though are minnows and crayfish, followed by nymphs like wigglers-perch bugs-caddis larvae, and sand worms. Worms, grubs, and leeches take their share, but in all honesty, the other morsels do far better under most circumstances day in and day out.

Spring Fishing

Once the ice goes, we humans decree the spring angling season open, although most waters see the perch moving to the shallows before the ice goes. The sun on open water just speeds things up a bit.

Unlike bluegills and crappie, perch do not bunch up as much in the shallows to spawn as a rule. Rather, they are more likely to spread out over the shoals and flats, given the choice of a large enough area to work with. This fact correlates with the minimal amount of vegetation they prefer to drop eggs in and around at this early, slow growth, cool water period.

Since anglers are likely to run across groups of fish made up of perhaps a dozen or so, here and there, a definite advantage is to put one's mind in a constant search frame so the temptation to set in one spot long is preempted. That leads to employing several options, search rigs if you will, to efficiently aid in that endeavor.

Given a favorable wind, drifting is a fine way to scour the flats for spring perch, especially if there are two anglers in the boat. Slip bobber setups, baited with small minnows like bluntnose, emeralds, spottails, or fatheads can be left to drag while casting small jigs tipped with wigglers or crayfish tails. This way, anglers can cover areas to either side of the boat, as well as the rear in case fish move in behind, after the boat has passed. If anglers find themselves lacking "natural" motor power, boat movement is best handled by either and electric or oars. Noisy gas engines will spook fish, as will both graphs and sonars left on in shallow water on occasion, particularly in those heavily fished lakes.

The somewhat smaller he fish will remain on the flats for a time after spring egg laying, with the ladies preferring to work along the first major breaklines. Those seeking these larger perch should work within casting distance of that bottom change while up on the flats so that both areas can be covered adequately.

Summer Fishing

Once waters get into the mid to upper 50's bracket, figure on fishing nearer to the lake basin as perch will be moving into the summer period. Primary spots are likely to be points, bars, and other drop offs, as well as sunken islands, in the 15-25 foot levels. Later on this depth range will shift even deeper so that by the middle of summer, the largest fish are usually found near the 30-50 foot level. That is if and until Mother Nature steps in.

Those deeper lakes, the ones that are known for the best perching, often undergo what is termed stratification in the dog days of late summer, usually late July, August, and early September. The term describes a layering of water into three levels; the epilimnion, metalimnion or thermocline, and the hypolimnion. Of these three, the hypolimnion is the bottom layer where temperature is coolest, most stable, and lowest in oxygen content. At the opposite end of the scale, the upper strata of water, is the epilimnion with slowly dropping temperatures as depth increases and adequate oxygen levels for the fish. The dividing line between these two zones where temperature drops rapidly is the thermocline, in essence the dividing line between livable and non-livable water for the perch.

Naturally, all lakes do not thermocline, and some stratify less drastically than others, thus allowing some fish activity below the thermocline. Among those most likely to allow this condition are the very young lakes geologically speaking. The point of the matter is that during mid-summer, such a condition can restrict how deep the perch can go, say a thermocline at 35 feet for example. That eliminates a lot of area for anglers to search if they know it exists, hopefully making fish contact both easier and quicker. Towards the end of recognizing this stratification, a temperature gauge such as the Lowrance Fish-N-Temp with its corded thermometer is a boon to summer perchers.

Once anglers have determined the extent of stratification and the levels affected, the next stop is to find out where the perch are located in conjunction with it. There are few better rigs than a bell sinker (dipsey) with tandem hooks above the weight at eight and eighteen inches respectively. Trolled or drifted along the likes of sunken islands, points, or what have you at the appropriate level of depth until the fish are found will work exceptionally well. Once agreeable perch are discovered, these rigs can be cast and retrieved through the area from an anchored boat or set fished on the bottom.

The main reason for employing a tandem rig for perch is to take advantage of that gluttonous nature mentioned earlier. The hypothesis works whether you are tossing jigs or rigs, or jigging ice spoons. Once one has a perch on the end of a line, not being too hasty in hauling the fish in will pay dividends. Rather, let him swim around with his brethren a bit. That wildly flapping second bait is sure to attract added attention, as evidenced by the number of times a fish will be followed right to the boat by several kin intent on stealing a meal when using only a single hook.

Figure 29. Tandem rigs, whether jigs, rigs, or ice spoons, take advantage of the gluttonous nature of the yellow perch.

As for the live baits involved in such fishing, perch are not overly picky that is for sure. With summer at peak, nymphs and small crayfish do well. As always, minnows produce a goodly share of perch too. Leeches, waxworms, leaf worms, and at times catalpas are all worth trying also.

Autumn Perching

Fall fishing is apt to be some of the best of the year for perch fans. The breakup of the stratification process allows fish to go where they please in search of fat to help tide them over during the long, lean pickings winter. At this time, perch do just that, but as fall progresses, they seem to prefer steep fast drop offs where they can follow what is left of the now declining food chain. That left over is minnows like emerald shiners, spottail, or bluntnose baitfish, who are also limited as to what they get to eat, namely plankton.

With sun angles declining, most of the warmth is concentrated along north shorelines, and that same angle effect keeps waters darker than one might think. Plankton can afford to rise towards the surface even at mid-day on occasion, followed by the baitfish, and the perch.

In this time and location, vertical jigging is heads above all other presentations, although a slip bobber setup and dipsey rigs also take plenty of fish. Using some of the minnows mentioned, a plain ball jig in the eighth size makes the best sense for fishing over the side of the boat. The hook is run through the minnow's mouth and out through the back, which sets it naturally in the water. A soft up and down movement, a high lift and drop, or a circular jiggin motion will all make the combination appear in a manner close enough to the real thing as far as the perch are concerned.

This is likely to be suspended fishing, depending on both the plankton and baitfish, so some way to keep track of the level of your bait is a must. One of the better options is to mark the line before fishing. The easiest way of doing just that is to unspool a section in the yard or along the driveway, then measure off five and ten foot sections, marking them with a permanent felt pen. Start at the point where the jig will be tied on, and use one color for the five foot lines and another for the ten foot marks, up to say, fifty feet in length.

Winter Season

Once the ice locks things up, angling shifts back to deep water if the lake affords it, for all but the smaller fish. Seldom will you find the elders in water less than fifteen foot deep. Bait preferences run from wigglers and minnows to grubs that simulate plankton with a thyroid problem. Since perch are attracted to flash quite often, the use of attractor spoons is a good idea. With them, anglers can also make use of some of the grub baits like waxworms, wasp larvae, goldenrod grubs, spikes, and mousies too.

The same doubled-up hook rigs work for the same reason under the ice as they do in warmer times, particularly when small baitfish are added. In the winter, such setups will get a bait down faster too, which is a definite plus when it comes to taking advantage of aggressively feeding fish. Besides that, light line with only a single spoon or hook can make you old just watching it ever so slightly drop to the perch's level.

Winter perchers soon get used to doing a bit of searching during hardwater. With food chains so shortened, grazing is a lifestyle for the fish in winter. It is therefore a good idea to fish with a crowd if you can swing it. That way, anglers can spread out a bit to look for active fish, then converge on the spot. If they move, fishermen can disperse to begin looking again.

Figure 30. Black Crappies are primarily a fish of clear, cool waters common to the northern parts of the country.

Chapter 14

Crappie Craft

The fish with so many names is ideal for the bait fishing angler. Common handles include Specks, Lamplighters, Strawbass, Calico Perch, Papermouth, and Bachelor Perch just to mention a few. All refer to Crappies, both the white and black variety, indigenous to just about every part of the nation in this day and age.

You can expect to do some respectable crappie catching in waters that range from reservoirs to lakes and rivers, although in the latter it will be in sections with little current. Among the two species, White Crappie, *Pomoxis annularis*, prefer larger water than that of their cousins the blacks, and are more tolerant of turbidity and higher temperatures. In addition, they are also a more prolific breeder than blacks.

Black Crappie, *Pomoxis nigromaculatis*, are primarily a fish of clear, cool waters more common to the northern areas of the country. While both species are what you could term "open water" fish — those that can readily operate suspended and away from structure — they are not so in the truest sense of the phrase like salmon for instance. Rather, while often found out and away, it is in relation to the likes of points, sunken islands, bars, creek beds and debris, according to each species' preferences. Along those lines, black crappie like weedlines, rock bars, and humps with firm bottoms, while whites get by with soft turf and sunken timber, logs, or submerged treelines like those common to many reservoirs.

Both species can and do inhabit the same waters on occasion, which often leads to some confusion of the part of anglers. The differences, while not startling, are sufficient enough to make a definite determination however. One of the primary tattletail characteristics between fish is the dorsal fin where whites display six spines while blacks have from 7-8 dorsal spines. Other aberations come in the way of markings and coloration. White crappie are more silver with definable vertical bars on the sides. Blacks, true to their name, show dark, mottled and irregular markings on their flanks, and their backs are more distinctly arched than those of their relatives. They are also of a stockier build.

Both fish have roughly the same spawning habits, laying eggs in water from 3-8 feet deep once temperatures near the mid sixty range very near cover. For whites, that means brush piles, bushes or sunken logs. Blacks like reeds or other weeds. However, both crappies are not all that particular when it comes to a bed site, taking whatever happens to be available, even if not optimum condition wise.

As for food, crappies will take baitfish above all else given the choice, but will not turn down nymphs and small crayfish, nor will they bypass a juicy wriggling leafworm or catalpa in season. In the evening hours, terrestrial such as a misplaced cricket or grasshopper will also get their attention as they move towards the shallows at times.

Spring fishing may start as early as January down south, as late as April in the north country. In the latter, there may a great deal of pre-spawn angling in the channels and bays due to early ice out, but still too cold of a water temperature for spawning to draw near.

The best channels for early crappie pursuit enclose the following conditions. Dark bottoms on the northern sides of lakes to get the most benefit from prevailing sun angles just like early bluegilling is a must. So too are channels that dead end to minimize current flow that can draw off warm water. There should also be plenty of shore cover to provide a wind break and some bottom hideouts for the fish as well. These are the ones that will draw the crappie's favorite forage first, minnows. Good bays, should channels be non-existent or not adequate, have basically the same criteria for good early fishing.

Forage being what it is, one does not have to be a Rhodes Scholar to figure out a successful bait for this time of the year. Still fishing slip bobbers with minnows from a channel or bay bank can produce lots of fish. Close in, anglers can use little more than a can or fiberglass pole. Reaching crappies further out will require a spin or spincast outfit. Either way, with cold water temps, a single hook and virtually no action other than that which the minnow provides will do the most good.

Later on, as things finally warm up, crappie fishers will find the fish responding to a tiny jig and minnow or spinner and minnow, especially as the fish prepare to begin the reproduction rites. Aggressive and belligerent over their territory, they attack such offerings with a vengeance. The females, which can weigh much more than two pounds in some waters with a bellyful of eggs, are not quite so energetic, but eat often enough to suck down a jig and minnow suspended under a bobber retrieved stop and go style.

One fun way to get spawning crappies is dabbling for them with minnows, leeches, small crabs, nymphs, or streamers tipped with a bit of worm. The technique is a favorite in the south using a cane pole and short line. The object is to locate productive areas then sneak close enough to allow the bait to be dropped vertically near the beds. Expect a hot welcome, and use polarized glasses so as not to miss the fish or his response.

Summer Techniques

Crappies during the warmer months exhibit that roaming, more open water nature, white to a greater extent than blacks. Since baitfish remain their high priority eating material, this is pretty much a necessity. However, on many waters minnows often move inshore once the sun starts to set after spending the bright hours suspended offshore.

Locating crappies is about 75% where you begin. They like to lay off the inside bends of points and bars during midsummer, and will relate to obstructions such as brush piles if they exist. Using a lake map to spot sunken islands, saddles, and the like will be a big help. Often times, this is where the elders of the tribe will gather.

Those crappies, especially whites, inhabit reservoirs like the outside bends of old creek channels, and if the area was left uncleared when the reservoir was filled, so much the better. Normally, there will be lots of brush left with the trees that will attract baitfish, and the crappie right along with them, staying until the forage leaves. In order to pinpoint fish under any of the locational patterns involved, anglers will have to do some looking, and one of the best rigs for live baiters is nothing more than a spinnerblade added just above a plain hook.

This hunt rig can be trolled behind either a bottom walking sinker or a couple of shot, depending on how high or low the fish are holding. Choose the blade according to water conditions, and in the heavier cover use a light wire hook in order to pull loose in case of hang ups. Once crappies are located, then it's time to switch to a couple of other time honored methods to fill coolers and live wells.

One of the very best ways to pursue summer crappies is at night, using the same means and principle mentioned in the capture of open water emerald shiners after the sun goes down. In essence, what anglers will be doing is setting things up so another member of the food chain, namely crappies, are present along with the baitfish. The better catches from the use of this method seem to come from the 18-25 foot depth levels, which give these panfish room enough to set up their traditional pecking order, common when groups of them get together.

Using one of the twelve volt battery powered floating lights, either commercial or homemade, anchor near to or right on the edge of the spot where the crappies were located earlier. Plan on fishing two rigs, four if there are two anglers, so that a dual approach can be made. One rod can be fished with a small slip bobber while the other is put to work casting or fishing vertically, preferably

Figure 31. A dual approach fished under a floating spotlight using a slip bobber and minnow - jig/minnow is the best presentation for night fishing.

with a jig and minnow combo. After a short while, the baitfish should be readily visible below the light as they feast on plankton, and the crappies will not be far behind.

The trick to taking the largest fish is determining at what depth bracket the school is located. Crappies will school vertically, sometimes a foot off the bottom at the start of the evening and rising as the night goes on. In any case, what size fish you are catching will help determine this, as the oldsters will let the youngsters do most of the work, laying back and feeding off the easy pickings of crippled, stunned, or dis-oriented baitfish that drift down to them at the base of the school. Therefore, if you are catching small to medium sized fish, try a little deeper until contact is made with the big fish.

Another very good approach for summer crappies is to work your own fish magnets, given the legality of such man made structures in your waters. Sinking the likes of old christmas trees, brush piles, or perhaps discarded tires will create whole communities of underwater life from algae and plankton to baitfish and crappie. Such deviations on the bottom in areas formerly devoid of structure can create real hotspots for crappiers to work day or night, and seasonally too, if they take into mind the locational patterns of the fish.

Fall Patterns

As water temperatures dip with the season, each species of fish react a little differently to those changes. Often there is an initial feeding spree at the onset of such changes, then a shift to different areas and a slowdown as winter approaches. Black crappies are more active than whites during the fall, which is no surprise since they prefer cooler waters anyway. Watch for them to move into the shallows to feast on the last remnants of insects, nymphs, crawdads, and baitfish as the leaves brown up right after the turnover in the north.

This is a good time to drift the flats with a long pole for live baiters, particularly around left over weed beds. Just keep flipping the float and bait ahead of the moving craft, allowing the bobber to come even with the boat and repeat. Thin wire hooks or the egg variety

variety dressed with wigglers, stone or dragonfly nymphs, tiny craws or the ever standard minnow are standard bait choices for the maneuver. Keep one good eye on the float though as crappies often will just tip it over on its side as if the rig has settled on the bottom because of a too deep depth setting. What will actually be happening is that some hungry crappie has risen to mouth the bait.

Where reservoirs and thus primarily white crappie are the mainstay of fall fishing, look for the silver panfish to head for creek and river channels. As things turn downright cold as winter gets near, they will drop right down into them. Steep breaks like the ones on outside bends and holes where a feeder steam or two entered the river before filling are both excellent choices to contact fish.

With water in such locations normally being deep, tight lining is the best bet for control and feel. Tandem hook setups will not hurt the fishing any. Both shot and bottom of the line-tied bell sinkers are all live baiters need to get offerings where the lamplighters are likely to be. As for bait? Well, whites being whites, fishermen can hardly go wrong with minnows.

Winter Ways

Crappies during the winter months are one of the most reliable species anglers can give chase to. Down south, fishing is pretty much handled the same way as it was through latter stages of the autumn season. As for blacks and northern waters, more than likely live baiters will have to swap boat oars for an ice spud and fishing through an ice hole.

The prime activity for crappies under the ice tends to be a constant search for food, concentrated at daybreak, sunset, and after dark when light penetration is at its minimum. In the very clear waters normal to winter, this is probably when they see the greatest advantage over their primary baitfish prey, as well as in tune with the biological clocks of the plankton, who are food for the minnows.

Winter crappie anglers will score more often, on more fish, if they follow a couple of rules. First off, carry an extra lantern and set it close to the ice holes being fished. Light through the ice attracts plankton almost as well as in the warmer months after dark.

Number two is to fish with a group whenever possible. The more bait being offered in a small area, the better the chances of holding a school of winter crappie once they move in, and try to fish with twin spoons per line.

Winter crappies will bite on baits other than minnows on occasion, even though it may sound odd given the minimal food chain and other forage possibilities. Mousies, wigglers, freshwater shrimp, waxworms, corn borers, wasp and bee larvae as well as other nymphs all do well when combined with tiny ice spoons. When anglers do choose baitfish, there are a couple of wrinkles worth putting to use. In order to make the minnows struggle more, appealing to the crappies basest predator instincts, try clipping the bottom section of the caudal or tail fin. This throws the minnow off kilter as it tries to swim, creating a constant stream of undulating wiggles that is of interest to the ever opportunistic crappie. Another way to go about the same task is to place the hook in the body section near the tail, thus hanging the minnow upside down in the water.

All in all, winter crappieing does not differ a whole lot from summer fishing other than the conditions faced by the fishermen, and alteration in tackle. The larger fish still shy away from active hunting if they can help it, preferring to gobble up the easiest eating. Mouths do not toughen up any, so ice anglers will have to play their fish deftly to avoid hook tearouts. Bobbers often just keel over in the confines of the ice hole from fish who take the bait on the rise, and the fishing is primarily one of suspension, since the crappies are not bottom huggers for the most part. Finally, productivity is as good or better under the confines of the ice, so there is really no reason to stay home and get cabin fever.

Chapter 15

Smalljaw Plots

Most often, there develops a love affair between man and fish once anglers are exposed to the Smallmouth Bass. Of course, the fish are not overly fond of the relationship, showing their disdain by using airborne tactics resembling a buzz bomb with a faulty gyroscope, or power runs that most locomotives would be proud of. Even when lip-locked by a lucky angler, they quiver with energy just waiting to break the grip and gain freedom once more. Then there is that fiery red eye, belligerently wishing some malady like the angler's arm going to sleep might strike at that moment.

God must make the best things in only small numbers so that when one happens upon them they are appreciated more. Of that, Mr. Smallmouth is a prime example. Compared to other species, smallies are rare in numbers quite simply because their needs and requirements for life are rigid. Primarily considered a stream fish when waters offer moderate to rapid flow, plenty of oxygenation and cool temperatures, along with clean, hard bottoms; smallmouth can and do inhabit lakes and reservoirs as well.

Originally, smallmouth were part of limited watersheds in Minnesota and Quebec south to Northern Alabama, and west to Kansas and Oklahoma. The birth of the railroad let fisherfolk east of the Alleghenies in on the Bronzeback's graces, and the Iron Horse finally brought them to California as well some years later. Still, they are not near as common as their largemouth cousins, although it could be said they are nationwide.

Given a choice, smallmouth anglers who wish to catch many bass, rather than just some bass, are better off employing a mixed bag of live bait morsels. *Micropterus dolomieui* just seems to prefer it that way, naturally, food wise that is.

The Spring Season

Smallmouths first get their fins itchy for some activity in the spring when water temperatures near the mid-forty mark. Sticking to rivers first will generally put fish in the boat long before lakes will. Warm runoff from the spring rains and subsequent feeder stream inflow is the reason.

Given the option, smallies will quite often eat crayfish before anything else, but at this juncture of the year, most of them will still be inactive compliments of the winter cold. The alternative is baitfish, both for the bass and the bass fisherman.

As with other species, early spring means slow presentations to match the mood of these bass. One route to a full stringer, especially where a lot of bottom debris or rocks are present, is to go with a slip bobber in order to suspend the minnow above such clutter. Another aspect of the float approach is that most of the smallies will be away from the heaviest current areas like riffles, due also to slow blood, opting instead for eddies and holes with a slower flow.

There is not a lot to this minnow fishing. Suspended under the bobber for depth adjustment when needed, a 2-3 inch chub or fathead is hooked through the lips, or under the dorsal fin, kept down with a couple of split shot. It is then just a matter of letting the minnow drift around doing his thing until a hungry enough smallmouth decides he has seen enough.

Cold water does not mean that minnow dunking is the only

way to go. Indeed, there are some artificial picks that bring bass, but they will need a little window dressing, enticement if you will, and still a slow approach if you want to take smallies with any consistency. Actually, what is being talked about here is the use of jigs; hair, rubber, or grub bodied. The second rule of thumb — first being the bait addition — is to pick just a heavy enough lead-head to reach bottom or near it according to water conditions, with a small sized body. That fact is classic smallmouth lore. They ususaly prefer something on the less than large size, often ignoring big food altogether.

How does one work jigs early on for smallmouth? In a matter of speaking you really do not, and that holds for fishing lead jigs in rivers or lakes, as well as at other times of the year. Far more smallmouth will be picked up trying to pick off a lead-head as it slides, glides, or is otherwise slowly, but steadily moved. Violent hops and jerks just do not get it, as modern verbiage might describe the hasty retrieves and their results where bronze bass are concerned.

By the time things get activated well on rivers, lake smallmouths ought to be turning on, moving from their near lake basin hibernation spots towards the first major breaklines.

Smallmouth in lakes are homebodies; born, living, and dying in the same general vicinity through generations if conditions remain constant. Once located, anglers can rely on the fact that the fish not inclined to having moved off somewhere, and all they have to do is figure out the routine that will produce during the time at hand. That is also a good reason why smallmouths are particularly suited to catch and release if anglers want to preserve their fishing over time.

Lake smallies have their preferences when it comes to living quarters among the various underwater structures. Since the waters they usually do well in encompasss those very young to middle aged geologically, likely real estate would include points, bars, rock humps, and islands both above and below the surface. To be productive where bronzebacks are concerned, they all will share hard bottoms, suitable spawning habitat close by (sand/gravel mixed flats), and a usable food source on hand (crayfish/minnows). The structures will also have to be tied directly with the lake basin and deep water to be used during the cold water period.

The first major move from winter lethargy sees lake smalljaws shifting from the basin to steep drop offs along some of the previously named structures in order to be close to the shallows. Still deep however, in the 30-40 foot range, live bait in the form of minnows fished with slip sinkers and light wire hooks or perhaps cork jigs is the optimum approach. It's a must to keep things slow, almost vertical at times, and small chubs, shiners, bluntnose, and fatheads are likely minnow picks.

As waters get to the upper forties to low fifties, things get going in a hurry on smallmouth waters. By then the crayfish will be coming out in force, and the bass will be heading onto the flats to greet them. Depth ranges from six to fifteen feet are well covered when baiters put jigs dressed with either baitfish or crayfish to work. Smallies often will take a whack at leeches and nymphs fished in this manner too. Slip bobbers are still an option, and have the advantage of picking up roaming bass in the opposite direction, meaning that anglers toss them out the opposite side of the boat from where they are jigging, or off the stern.

As spawn gets close in rivers or lakes, water temperatures in the upper fifties, aggression is the rule rather than the exception. Throw anything near territory staked out by a he fish and the bass will make Godzilla look like a chameleon. Two top notch angles are to pitch a crawdad or waterdog, both of whom have reputations as nest predators and are therefore natural enemies. Minnows with a single hook and shot dragged into the neighborhood will bring swift retribution also. As for the females, after the initial run onto the shallows early on, they will have dropped back to the first major breakline off the spawning flats awaiting hormone levels to peak, which send them onto the beds after dark to deposit eggs.

When water temperatures get into the low sixties, it is time to lay off smallies until spawning is over. Fish up north are generally mature enough to handle those biological needs at three years. Down south it is usually around two. She fish lay from 2-7000 eggs per pound of body weight, which will hatch in 2-10 days, depending on the weather. A five pound smallmouth therefore can render perhaps 35,000 eggs, not a lot when you consider their chances of surviving to like size in their world. Smallies need all the help they can muster, which includes a decrease to zero in angling pursuit while they are on the beds.

Summer Smalljawing

After the rigors of spawn, look for a recovery period of a week or two on most waters. Fishing in rivers after that is relatively easy compared to hunting smallmouths in lakes. There are a couple of basic reasons for this phenomena. River bass strike first and look later simply because the medium in which they live is one of constant motion. The faster that movement, the more likely it is that a moment's hesitation at the chance of a meal will cause a miss and empty stomach as the prey streaks off aided by the current.

Water movement has its hand in another area, that of where the smallmouth lives. That fact effectively eliminates unproductive water for those anglers who know what to look for.

Even the strongest species of fish cannot hold up for long periods in moving water, unless they use something to block or at least slow down current flow, giving themselves a respite. Over-exertion produces a buildup of lactic acid in their body muscles, much the same as we humans after lifting weights or something equally as strenuous. In fish however, it is quite often fatal, hence the need for cover. Along those lines, river fishermen can expect to find bass in the vicinity of anything that appears to retard or reduce flow. Islands, sand and gravel bars, rip-rap, bridge abutments, logs, rocks, and downed trees are some good examples.

Putting these bits of information together gives live bait fishermen a good idea of just what to use in moving water, as well as where to look. For quarter casting that allows baits to drift past likely bass hideouts, an inline spinner makes good sense. The likes of leeches, worms, grasshoppers, and nymphs strung on the light wire hooks are good selections for the method. For the fastest flows, pick one with willowleaf blades. Moderate flows can be fished with an Indiana blade, and for slower waters use a Colorado style.

Such pursuits as live bait fishing in waters that get from one place to another rather quickly lends itself to a more standard drift fishing style also. Setup with a three-way swivel, appropriate weighted dropper line, and snell with hook; live morsels from crayfish and nightcrawlers to nymphs and minnows will work this way. It is all quite natural, with the sinker barely ticking bottom while the current carries the bait at a natural pace downstream past a bass lair.

For mid-summer smallmouthing in lakes, live bait is hard to beat. The bass will move deep as conditions let them, often avoiding pursuit by almost all artificial enthusiasts other than plastic worm men and jig fishermen.

Here, the slip sinker and trolling or backtrolling approach is king, with a wrinkle or two. One of these is to add a small spinner blade in front of the bait, be it baitfish, leech, crawler or nymph. Veterans keep blade style in mind, as well as color to fit the situation. In extremely clear water for example, silver may not be all that great since too much flash will often put smallies on their guard. Copper might be better, as will colored blades. Off colored water lends itself to gold, chartreuse, orange, and a hammered effect, along with louder sound to let the bass know the dinner bell is on.

Keep in mind snell length, and anglers can also make use of cork heads to advantage with either minnows, waterdogs, leeches, and crawlers as well. Surprisingly enough, two cork floats well known to steelheaders will take their share of smallies too. Either spin-n-glos or wobble-glos are best married with leeches or night-crawlers.

One other alley worth exploring is the use of crayfish by a method affectionately known as, "Walking A Craw". The recipe calls for selecting a lively specimen of the lobster clan, pincers intact, and hooking from below the jaw up through the nose so that the hook point comes out between and just in front of the eyes. Too far back will hit the brain, and presto! Dead crab. A dropper, which can be a simple loop knot tied into the line about six inches in front of the crayfish, is then fixed with a single split shot, usually size 3/0.

In the water, the rig lets the crab do what comes naturally, scuttling around if you will. If he backs under a rock or some other debris trying to shirk his duty, steady pressure will walk him right back out into the open again. A slow retrieve will keep him strolling back towards the boat, grabbing the line with his claws rather than every obstruction he gets near. Tied up this way, it also makes

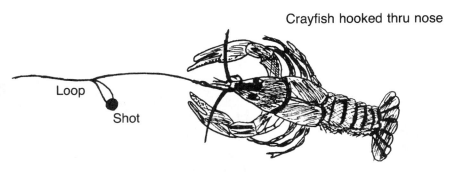

Crayfish hooked thru nose

Loop

Shot

Figure 32. "Walking Crawdad Rig"

things easy for Mr. Smallmouth, who can sneak up from behind then down the hatch. It works on bigmouths as well.

Autumn Smallies

Fishing for smallmouths is usually full swing by the time water temperatures dip into the mid 60's range. For a short time, while the food stuffs are still plentiful, action is likely both deep and shallow. Live bait tossers can put to use just about all that has been discussed so far in appropriate areas and catch fish. After the initial active phase, things tend to get a little slow, the fish shift position, and anglers have to go to work.

Water temperatures in the 50's send smallmouths towards what will end up as being winter quarters, and in addition, they begin to school as well. Spots close to the lake basin will hold the best odds for taking smallies, such as sunken islands, humps, steep points, and areas along fast sloping shelves where hard to soft bottom, clay to rock, and other changes occur. Also, by this time, expect food chains to be shortened once again, limiting forage choice and availability to the smallies.

The trick to getting bronze bass at this point is finding them. Backtrolling, controlled drifting, or just plain slow trolling are a must on all but the most familiar waters. However, under each mode, live bait fishermen get a fair choice of ways and means to present their offerings.

Figure 33. Spots close to the lake basin offer the best odds for fall smallies once waters drop below the fifty degree mark.

Vertical fishing is one of these, using either minnows to tip jigs, or a common perch rig with its twin hooks, and bottom tied dipsey or bell sinker. An ice fishing rapala is another alternate, again tipped with a small baitfish like a fathead. The previous rigs can also be baited with a nymph or crayfish, but in all cases, there is not a whole lot to the effort other than barely lifting the setup off the bottom rhythmically. The key is quiet, which means no large motor noise, little use of the electric, and no banging around the boat like a pachyderm with a hot foot. Plain drifting is perhaps best of all, if the wind allows it, that being the case.

Most of the time, the wind is not going to be that cooperative given the time of year, so some other plans have to be substituted when vertical fishing is out. Either trolling or backtrolling a slip sinker setup will do, but the rear movement will keep the boat moving slowest, which is more appropriate for the time of year and cold water conditions.

Once fish are found, anglers should not hesitate to anchor the boat and either set fish or cast. A slip bobber rig will do for no movement fishing, as will the sinker rig just simply left in place with only a move now and then. For casting, try a plain jig head in the fulcrum style, no body material, and with a number six hook if you can find one. The jig can be cast out, and line stripped off so that it settles as vertically as possible. Once on the bottom, it is then literally dragged back to the boat, or barely lifted then quickly dropped so that it moves in inches. As for live bait, both crabs and minnows are the better choices for the jig, ditto with the snell, but you can take some fish on occasion with an air injected worm if it is a small one.

There is one other thing that applies when fishing in the late fall, and that is to keep in mind that at this late stage of the game little things mean a lot, especially where smallies are involved. Keep an eye on the weather. A very clear, bright day with little wind will do wonders for the fishing, allowing sunlight to penetrate just enough to warm the water even a tad. That is all the smalljaws need to get a little active.

Winter Fishing

In the northern regions of smallmouth territory, where water will undoubtedly turn the consistency of concrete once the snow flies, fishing is for the most part over until spring. Both closed seasons and a hibernation-like state on the part of the bronzebacks being the chief reason. In more southern climes, fishing will still be available for those willing to leave the comfort of home and brave the chill. As for tactics, those that cover both the cold water periods of spring and fall will produce for live baiters once they figure out the wants of the fish in relation to their regional location.

Chapter 16

Largemouth Tactics

There is little argument that the Largemouth Bass is reigning monarch of American gamefish. Such notoriety espoused through everything from tee-shirts to media hype on the likes of television or through the words of outdoor writers keeps bass fishing at the top of the heap. Then again, bigmouths have been there for years anyway. The ultra modern mode for pursuit these days entails hunting bucketmouths with high speed boats, plastic baits, and sophisticated electronics. Chucking breathing baits for the most part, where his majesty is concerned, has gone the way of the cane pole for all but a few. By and large though, just as those early bassers well knew, live baits day in and day out are capable of outproducing the majority of other means by a wide margin.

Although largemouths are related to smallies, similarities do not go much farther beyond that. Largemouths fit into an almost entirely different environmental niche, preferring shallower waters on the whole, along with cover such as weeds, stumps, sunken logs, and flooded timber. With older, more fertile lakes, river backwaters, and some reservoirs providing such habitat, these are where bigmouths are most likely to thrive.

As far as land mass goes, largemouths can be found all over the country these days far from their indigenous roots that included southern Canada and the Great Lakes down the Mississippi Valley to Mexico and east to Florida. In the 1880's, they were introduced into the Columbia River System, and later traveled east into New England as well.

Spring Fishing

As with their cousins, fishing is greatly tied to the area of inhabitation. Fish in Florida can be considered pre-spawn conditioned from December until February, while their northern relatives are confined to darkness under ten inches of frozen water. Spring angling for yankee bass usually gets under way after ice out as water temperatures approach the upper forties.

The first lakes to try your luck on should be small and shallow, include a bay or two, perhaps channels, with dark mud or muck bottoms to hold heat. In that respect, they can be judged in the same manner as the ones one might select for crappies or bluegills. As for bait, those first trips to the shallows on the part of the bass are for the expressed purpose of alleviating the long winter's hunger pangs brought by shrunken food chains. Minnows and small panfish are the targets, hence baitfish the needed requirement to put bass on the hook.

Lethargy will still be somewhat of a problem, so the slowest presentation is best. That translates to letting the minnow do its thing, suspended from a slip bobber in most cases. If you want to get real tricky, an angler can also take an ice bobber in the half inch diameter range and snug it right up to the hook eye. A fair sized shot in the #3 to 7/0 size will take the bobber, #6 hook and baitfish to the bottom, hold it in place, yet allow the minnow to float off the bottom in plain sight of a hungry bass. Of course, the same results can be had with the aid of a floating cork jig head too. As for the baitfish choice? The earliest fishing is most profitable about a three inch fathead or chub. Later on, as waters warm just a bit, one can increase minnow sizes, allowing anglers to employ shiners too, up to four inches or so in size.

Figure 34. The first places that usually produce early spring largemouth are shallow bays, channels, and backwaters with dark bottoms that absorb heat.

As with other species, as spawn draws near, there will be a predominance of males in the shallows, and the he fish will be orienting themselves to firm bottomed areas such as sand or fine gravel/clay so they can begin fanning out the nest sites. Water temperatures in the low 60's are the key to such activity beginning. Once the nests are prepared, the males will select a female and herd her onto the nest where she may deposit up to 7000 eggs per pound of weight. She fish often drop eggs in more than one nest, especially if there are a large number of he fish. After the ordeal, largemouth ladies will usually move just off the first major breakline to recuperate for a time, from around 5-10 days or so.

Taking bass in large numbers is easy once spawn gets close, given the aggressive territorial nature of the males. Live bait rigs need not be sophisticated. A simple split shot and hook, appropriate in size and style to accommodate nightcrawler, leech, crayfish, or minnow; cast beyond, then slowly worked near will draw a quick response from Mr. Bass.

Summer Bigmouthing

After spawning, both males and females move into their summer habitats that can run from shallow water slop beneath the likes of lily pads and mossbeds to the edges of deep cabbage and coontail weedlines. Needless to say, just exactly where the bass are determines how they can be successfully approached and subsequently caught as well.

A time honored approach for bigmouths in the shallowest weedbeds and lily pads employs the use of live frogs. It is also likely to kick your ticker into overdrive like only one other thing that comes to mind.

Since bass chasers will be angling in what to amounts to a jungle, they will be needing some specific basics. Stout tackle in the category of a Shimano Crankin' Stick or perhaps a Flippin' Stick with a quality free-spool and 12 - 20 lb. test are called for. A must also will be weedless hooks such as Eagle Claws 249 series. As for the frogs, both leopards and green frogs will do fine, or small bull frogs as well.

What the method entails is working the holes and pockets common to most shallow water pad and weed patches. Bass like

Figure 35. Water temperatures in the 60's is the key to activity that sees the males entering the shallows to select nesting sites. Of concern to fall largemouths is what the weed growth is doing after the first heavy frosts and water turnover in natural lakes.

to lay in the cool shade around such openings, just waiting for an easy meal to wander within range. By casting beyond such openings, then working the frog into the open water, anglers will be giving bigmouths just that, frog a la carte. Expect the lake to explode open like someone set off a depth charge when your kicker clears the safety of the greenery, and once you set the hook, keep the head of the fish up and moving toward the boat. That is the precise reason for the heavy artillery.

Fishing the likes of cabbage weed presents several problems and needed options for live bait largemouth bassers, the first being just where in the greenery are the bass located. Contrary to a lot of popular thinking, that is not always at the base of the plants.

Quite often during periods of stable weather — three or four days worth at least with gentle winds — bigmouths will rise into the upper levels of the plants, suspending if you will. At the other end of the scale, following drastic cold fronts with clear bright skies that follow, bass go belly to the bottom, often burrowing head first into the weed growth. Now that is the "classic" negative mood. There are some that say the pressure change affects air bladders, which may indeed be true. The bottom line is that it is a condition summer bassers must expect and learn to cope with. Live baiters are the best equipped to do just that. Bait is the most dependable way to get fish after such changes.

Actual fishing under those really tough conditions is best done with the aid of either a slip sinker rig or small shot in conjunction with a weedless hooked leech or air injected nightcrawler. However, if pesky panfish are about, nix the worm and go with the leech to avoid the results of those nibbling attacks, which is no worm. Leeches can usually withstand the assaults, and save a lot of fishing time and bait.

The actual method is uncomplicated, being little more than letting the leech settle to the plant bases, and working it thru slowly in hopes of enticing a bigmouth, though inactive, to end its fast and suck the offering in.

The same setup will do fine for mid-depth weedline bass, especially if anglers will go to the lightest weight and work the leech so that it drops and flutters from plant to plant as the bait is raised and lowered on the retrieve, with a pause every now and then. Such presentations will see bass plucking the offering on the drop most often.

High riding, active bass, naturally give the bait tosser a better array of options. One of those is to use a small float, no weight, and a minnow allowed to frolic around above the weed tops. Frogs can be put to work in the same way, but in both cases, the object is to set the float shallow enough to keep the bait from using the greenery as a refuge from attack.

Casting crawlers or leeches in combination with a spinner blade is another way to put bass in the live well in relation to the weeds. Steady retrieves, but not too fast, will let the fish know something is on the way at roof top level which just might be edible. The slow, steady retrieve lets them home in on the blade vibration until they can sight the prey. With such bait and blade combinations, anglers have the choice of making their own or buying a commercial variety with either double or triple hooks. All will work well.

Blades and bait are also a good selection for anglers who like to get in a little night fishing for summer largemouth. Prime locales along the weedlines after dark are the tops, and both inside and outside edges. Trolling with an electric or oars is the best presentation and big blades do the most good since the fish will need plenty of noise to guide them in the black of night. On many lakes where daytime pressure is excessive, night fishing is the very best alternative if anglers want fish.

Autumn Angles

The key to taking fall largemouth is to watch the signs of the times, so to speak. After the first heavy frost and the initial upset of the turnover, things begin to change rapidly. Of primary concern to the bass is what the weed growth is doing, hence the bass chaser as well.

As the shallower water weeds die off, a migration of sorts towards deep water begins for some bass. The process is indeed a gradual one that sees those pad and moss bed fish move into the flats where the ravages of lessening sunlight and frost have not yet had their effect. There, they join other bass, those resident fish already living there. As these deeper cabbage beds die off in turn, bass move to others still in good shape, leading to larger and larger groups of fish in each area of the lake until finally — winter just around the corner — they all move into the depths near the lake basin. Thus, the key to fishing autumn for largemouths is finding still green weeds. Presentations and bait choices for the period are fairly wide for live baiters due to the range of conditions entailing bass behavior in this time of change.

Early on, just about everthing can trigger a positive response as fish are still charged up due to fairly warm waters, and the need to store up fat for winter. That spinner and crawler setup trolled through the flats is one good bet, and leeches are a deadly substitute for the worms too. Try drifting a minnow under a slip bobber over submerged weeds while casting a jig and minnow, leech, or salamander to work the plant bases at the same time as additional ploys to put fall bigmouths in the boat as well.

As things cool off more and more, activity is often tied to the weather on a given day, but live baiters will be affected far less than artificial pitchers. Because the sun angle has shifted far enough south, bright calm days will produce fish in greater quantities as the season wanes into winter. Still, metabolism not being what it once was, anglers have to slow down a bit.

A great way to take bigmouths once they are congregated on the last green seed stands is with the marriage of spinner bait and minnow. Big single spins will allow for the slowest bring back yet allow the blades to revolve, flashing and putting out that steady vibration that attracts fish. With these oversized blades, bass hunters can also let their bait and blade marriage helicopter up and down the remaining weed walls and take bass, especially those less active fish not inclined to move far for a meal.

The coldest period before ice up can be tough on both fish and fishermen. Activity will be minimal, the weed growth all but gone, and the bass moving to their winter quarters. Bassers can figure on fishing in waters from 15-25 feet deep or better, which means they will have to get specific with presentations in order to catch fish. One of the best ways is to fish vertically and slowly

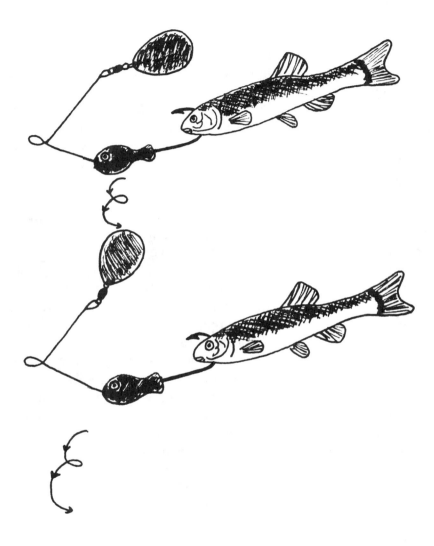

Figure 36. Helicoptered Spinner-Bait

with small minnows, either on the likes of a small eighth ounce without a bulky body, or a split shot, hook, and baitfish setup, with or without a float, and a small one at that.

Winter Fishing

Once things settle into the pattern, winter angling seems to pick up a bit for largemouths, and is fairly good throughout the season down south; for at least the first half up north.

The mainstay of live baiting below the Mason-Dixon line is large shiners or salamanders worked under a cork float near to or in weedgrowth. Up north, fishing through hard water with baitfish is the best bet too, but on a smaller scale minnow wise, and with a couple of different approaches, due of course to the frozen H_2O.

Although some fishermen have been known to use summer sized outfits which will work, scaled down spinning and free-spool outfits work much better for bassing through the ice. The rods usually are no longer than 36 inches in either version, and can be used to jig or bobber fish. Minnows in the 2-3 inch size work best, and can be fished with a small hair jig in the eighth to sixteenth ounce range. Winter bassmen can also employ standard jigging baits such as a small Swedish Pimple or Hopkins Spoon with the treble replaced by a single hook, bait fish attached to that.

Some of the best winter largemouth fishing comes on lakes with clear water, suprisingly enough. The reason for such success is due to the fact that some green weedgrowth can exist in the deeper water. Granted, it will not be much, and scattered at that, but what there is will attract both bait and panfish, which serve bigmouths well as tablefare in the winter months.

Strikes by largemouth under the ice very often are more savage than those of summer, which is probably both a result of the fact that other fish are the designated dinner, and they can not afford to miss, given the scarcity of food. Such assaults can fool anglers into thinking the fish are more active than they are, and speed the action of their baits up a bit. This is generally a no-no. Keeping it slow and varied with plenty of long pauses will outproduce other action, and if anglers pay attention, they will find that most of those hard strikes occur while the bait is at rest.

Chapter 17

Walleye & Sauger Methods

Both walleye and sauger are hard hunted by a great many fishing fanatics, not so much for the fight once hooked, but rather on the platter. The fact that both fish seem to be a bit of a problem catching wise for many of the angling fraternity holds an allure in itself. They can be persnickety and elusive unless one fully understands their habits in both the lakes and rivers which they inhabit. For the novice though, the use of live bait will be a big help towards putting fish in the boat, and subsequent filets on the plate.

Both species are relatives to the yellow perch, although far different in appearance from that relative. As for the pair considered together, they are similar enough to fool even some veteran anglers not completely familiar with the distinctions.

Stizostedion vitreum vitreum is the scientific label for the largest member of the family of perch, which is the walleye. Saugers are *Stizostedion canadense*, smaller on the average by quite a ways, and not nearly as wide spread. While walleyes have been stocked in many areas successfully, lakes as well as rivers; planted saugers do not fare nearly as good. It seems that saugers survive in only

Figure 37. Saugers do better in large water systems like the Great Lakes, Mississippi, Ohio, Missouri, and Tennessee Rivers.

the largest of waters like the Great Lakes, and the cool large bodies of southern Canada, along with big rivers systems such as the Mississippi, Missouri, Ohio, and Tennessee. In moving water habitats, they show a preference for the darker, more turbulent conditions than their cousin, even though both are known as Circadian (night active) or Crepuscular (twilight active) feeders primarily.

One of the best distinguishing features between the two is their coloration patterns, especially in the tail and dorsal fin. The tip of the walleye's tail has a milky-white coloration, absent completely in the sauger. Where the dorsal fin is concerned, clearly definable spots on the fin are characteristic of the sauger, while walleyes exhibit a dark spot at the base of the last two or three spines of that fin. As for that smaller than average size of the sauger just mentioned, they average perhaps a pound and a half with a six pound fish being considered trophy material. Walleyes can reach up to twenty pounds, and as for a wall hanger, fish of ten pounds will meet that requirement.

The great thing about this pair is that anglers who do well on one have the built in know how to catch the other in almost all waters, given their almost identical life styles.

Spring Fishing

Even with seasonal opening and closing dates set by an individual state's DNR, walleye fishing can be considered good just about all year, even though the angler may consider conditions a little less than tolerable where he or she is involved. Walleyes begin their congregations for spawning in January/February, though ice has covered rivers or lakes in the northern part of their range.

Males are the first to reach the future spawning sites, followed by the she fish as waters get into the 40's. Actual egg laying will take place when those temperatures get to around 47-49 degrees, and the female can produce from 25-70,000 eggs per pound of body weight.

The right turf varies, depending on what the fish have available, from prime rock and gravel to flooded marsh grass. The ritual itself will take place after dark with the female randomly dropping eggs across the spawning area, accompanied by several males who will be depositing milt at the same time. No distinguishable nests are involved, nor protection of the eggs or young, who will hatch out anywhere from 12-20 days later, depending on water conditions and temperature. During the period right up to actual fertilization males are far more aggressive than lady walleyes, and thus easy targets for live baiters who take into consideration the cold water temperatures and resulting metabolism.

Without a doubt, minnows will take far more fish in the early pre-spawn period than anything else. In rivers, one of the best ways to present them is in conjunction with a jig. A second choice would be the slip sinker rig with a bottom walking style of weight due to the normal debris strewn along the bottom of such waters.

In either case, the technique of slipping is a good tool for locating holding spots, particularly when the changing water levels involved in spring river fishing are about. To "slip a river" one needs a boat, preferably equipped with a motor, although in times past oars had to do. The object is to keep the boat moving with just enough force upstream to let the current carry the boat backwards downstream. Although the description sounds like a contradiction in terms, it does work, letting anglers cast, troll, or vertical fish all at once if there are three in the boat, and more importantly, in a slow methodical manner.

Spring walleye chasers can usually count on fish being found in certain areas in relation to the current flow just mentioned. Before heavy run off from spring rains occur, dam sites become magnets for walleyes headed upriver to spawn, barriers that they are. The spot to usually find fish during bright daylight hours is the main washout hole directly below the gates, and its edges as long as there is slack water. After dark or at other low light periods, the flats immediately below the hole at the downstream base of the apron where the walleyes can hunt minnows, particularly around large rock and other bottom deviations.

Figure 38. Before heavy run off from spring rain occurs, dam sites on rivers are walleye magnets for fish headed upriver to spawn.

When the high water from the opening of flood gates does commence, it blows the fish out from immediately below the dams. Where they go from there is either downstream or off to the sides if the area below the dam is wide enough. In any case, the key to fish holding spots is that they provide the walleyes with a safe respite from the heavy currents. Rip rap, flooded vegetation and brush, downed trees, and inlets along the bank are all likely to attract high water walleyes in a spring flood control situation.

Early walleyeing in lakes, like river fishing, should be keyed on pre-spawn and spawn behavior, which means slowed down presentations and specific locations. Since the fish eggs need some water movement to keep the future walleyes clean and well oxygenated, that can help somewhat. Inlets where streams enter a lake are probable drawing sites, as are marshes with the same source. Shoals and bars where wind can activate wave action for a sustained time are also walleye spawning grounds on some waters.

Live baiters will also find that the two presentations most useful in rivers will produce lake walleyes as well, but the slip sinker rig will outdo the jig and minnow. Another, slip bobber and baitfish is a good alternative too. Of course, slipping is out, but slow trolling, drifting, and back-trolling are not, as long as each is done to match those conditions so in control of the walleye and their behavior.

Lake fish are far more moody than their river cousins at this time of the year, which translates to difficult daytime angling. The alternative is to fish after dark, being thoughtful enough not to forget the snowmobile suit.

Either working from a boat or wading will get bait fishermen action after sunset as the walleyes move into the shallows to feed. Night fishermen also get to add one more wrinkle to their presentations schemes due to the unique vision tool walleyes are endowed with.

Due to the fact that walleyes are equipped with numerous rods, twin cones (compared with single ones for us humans), and special white reflecting cells, they see much better in dim light than many other animals. Hence their penchant for dining after dark when they have a distinct advantage. Bait anglers who will venture out after

Figure 39. Either wading or boat fishing will get action after sundown as walleyes head into the shallows of lakes to feed.

hours can employ a small spinner blade in front of a light wire hook and minnow with split shot for casting weight. The setup can also be trolled across the flats, acting in either case as both a light and noise disseminator that the walleyes will have no trouble homing in on.

Summer Tactics

After the rigors of spawning, things slow down for at least a couple of weeks as the fish recover their strength. River fish are the first to bounce back and move into the summer period. The larger schools will break down into smaller units, scatter downstream to summer haunts, and begin feeding regular again.

Among places to work on in summertime river walleyeing are downstream holes and washouts adjacent to the larger shallow water flats the fish visit after dark. Lacking such depressions in a stretch of river, walleyes will also use conventional current breaks such as boulders, stumps, and eddies found on the lee side of islands, points, and other land connected projections.

Although walleyes again will strike any of the aforementioned presentations, anglers can add still numerous others due to the warmer water and corresponding higher metabolic rate of the fish. Both drifted crawlers and nymphs like the wiggler will get walleyes as will a leech and wobble-glo or spin-n-glo fished behind a small rubbercore sinker. On occasion, they will also attack a crawfish. Weight forward inline spinners can also entice fish if quarter casted and left to swing in behind obstructions or into a hole on a tight enough line to keep the blade working.

As for lake walleyes, a great deal depends on what type of body of water anglers are fishing, being deep and natural, or stocked and shallower. Walleyes in such different environments must adapt their life styles to fit each, thus changing the angler's approach if he or she wants to catch fish that is.

Deep water fish force live bait anglers to employ primarily a back-trolling presentation for both speed control and maneuverability along points, sunken islands, humps, and sloping drop offs. Some change in the bottom is what the walleyes relate to when down in the deep, such as large to smaller rock, clay to muck and the like. Using one of the bottom walking sinkers will enable live bait fishermen to detect such aberrations to the best. The trick is to keep the line as vertical to the rod tip as possible for maximum feel. Proper sinker weight is as much a key as style. For waters from twenty-five foot to around forty select weights in sizes from 3/8 to 1/2 ounce, and beyond forty-five feet a 3/4 ounce is in order.

With the rest of the rigging involved with these sinkers, live bait users should bear in mind that deep water walleyes will suspend, especially when active, but perhaps not actually aggressive and feeding. Longer snells with air injected crawlers, spinner blade additions to the snell, and floating jig heads will all help to keep baits in view of such fish.

Live bait users should also be aware that summer walleyes show a definite preference for nightcrawlers during the hot months, followed by leeches, with minnows a distant third. The only other live bait that might compete with the worms where larger fish are present is waterdogs.

Live bait users should bear in mind too that deep water walleyes will suspend, especially when active although not actually aggressive and feeding. Longer snells with air injected crawlers, spinner blade additions to the snell, and floating jigs will all help to keep baits in view of the fish.

Many stocked lakes do not afford walleyes a deep water escape from summer brightness, and even some natural lake walleye populations use shallower water a great deal of the time. Where they go is into the weed beds during daylight hours, and walleye chasers have to go in after them if they want fish. Fortunately, live bait affords one of the best ways to do just that.

For bait, neither nightcrawlers or minnows is the best pick, given the presence of pesky panfish and the tough greenery the bait must traverse in its course. Instead, sturdy leeches can withstand both hazards far better, and with the addition of a #6 or #8 weedless hook, allow the angler to work the weeds efficiently. Another variation in the live bait rig is a change in sinkers from the standard bottom walker to a tapered worm sinker that will slip through the growth with less difficulty.

Fishing the weedbeds for walleyes is much the same as with

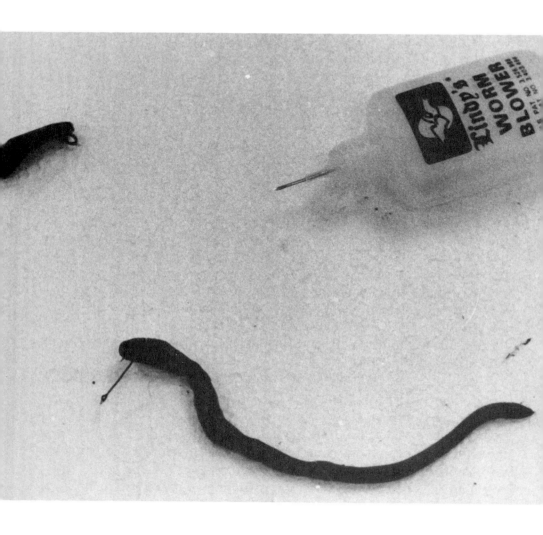

Figure 40. Longer snells with air injected nightcrawlers help keep bait in view of suspended fish at times.

largemouth bassing, the exception being that walleyes relate more to the bottom. Points of weeds, inside turns, depressions in the bottom, and openings in the growth are all variations in terrain that attract and hold fish, therefore warranting the attention of walleye anglers.

During the bright of the hot, sultry dog days of summer, weed beds can pay dividends for live bait fishermen if they will venture out beyond sunset also. Walleyes will move out of the thickest cover to forage on the shallow inside edges, as well as along the upper levels of the weeds if there is room between the surface of the lake and the plant tops.

Unlike daytime angling where casting to explore every nook and cranny is the best approach to fishing the weeds, night hours favor long line trolling with electric motors or oars for stealth. In-line spinners with leech or crawler such as the June Bug are great for such work. Double or triple hook nightcrawler harnesses with blades are as good for the conditions.

Fall Fishing
The change of seasons make little difference to either walleyes or knowledgeable anglers, both of whom can count on full activity from the other. In rivers, fishermen can expect a migration of sorts in stretches below dams as the walleyes move to the man made structures as waters cool. Some will drop back when winter does arrive, while others will remain throughout the cold water period.

Those fish too far downriver to heed the urge to move nearer to dams travel instead to the deeper holes for the winter. Usually the deepest ones are found on the outside bends, and should they be adjacent to a food shelf of substantial size, populations can be large and a sure thing for the angler.

Walleyes in lakes tend to change locations too, but moves are tied to forage more than anything else. One major prey species on the deeper lakes are cisco, which spawn in the late fall on rock and rubble shoals or bars next to deep water haunts. Egg laying takes place at night, and walleyes, some of them real monsters, are found in the same locations taking advantage of the rich, fatty food source.

Other night moves in waters that put walleyes within easy reach of wading anglers involves emerald shiners. Indeed, wading may be the only way to get at these fish on the best fishing nights which are characterized by plenty of wind, and quite often white-capped waters that would make fishing from a boat in the black of night hazardous to say the least.

Night angles on lakes for live baiters are pretty much limited as far as presentations are concerned. Jigs with twister tailed grub bodies for movement detection by the walleyes and baitfish add-ons for scent are the best producers. If anglers can see well enough from shore lighting, a slip bobber and minnow or salamander may add to stringer weights as well.

Daytime fishing is tied to forage factors too. On some waters, particularly those with some marshland close at hand, walleyes will be on the spot for frog migrations right around the first frost. A more reliable approach is to tie walleye chasing with the movements of the schools of yellow perch. Minus the deepwater cisco forage, perch are normally the primary food souce for walleyes on most waters.

Given the locations of perch after the turnover, live bait rigs with slip sinkers, worked along the steeper drop offs with waterdogs and chubs or shiners will do live bait fishermen the most good during daylight hours. Keeping in mind the sun angles, southern shores will be the darkest for the longest periods each day. With the walleyes distaste for bright, those spots located in that direction are likely to be more productive for longer periods throughout autumn.

Winter Walleyeing

Suprisingly enough, once things get downright cold, walleye-ing stays pretty hot for those willing to brave the elements. Fishing under the ice for mooneyes is as much a matter of when and where as how. The walleye's nature does not change much, other than to slow them down a bit with frigid waters and all. They still shun bright light, which means that sunny days will not see a whole lot of activity. Dusk and dawn however, are another matter.

Walleyes will still make forays to the shallows in winter, especially where perch in the 5-6 inch range are a major food source. The small panfish often hang around levels from 10-15 feet once the ice gets on, and the walleyes are not far off.

Presentations are limited once again. Trolling through an ice hole is considered by many as unproductive. Rather, set fishing with minnows is the preferred choice, making use of either mini-spinning outfits, like free-spool rigs, or the more standard tip-up.

Fishing with the rods is best done in conjunction with a tiny as practical slip bobber, paying particular attention to the stop. Both wire and plastic have a tough time functioning properly in the cold, and resetting depth levels often ends up with a twisted or broken line. Line stops made from dacron like the "Grabber" from RCG Products or Cassopolis, Michigan are far superior, sliding easily when the need arises.

With the lower metabolic rates of winter walleyes, baitfish like chubs, shiners, and fatheads need not be any larger than 3-4 inches. Clipping fins may help to attract walleyes and tickle their trigger into eating what appears to be an injured, therefore hapless dinner.

Locations in the winter can vary from lake to lake depending on the makeup of the bottom. Points, sunken islands, steep break-lines, flats, and the like can all give up fish at one time or another. Walleyes will do a lot of roaming in the winter due to the shortened food chain.

Fishing in rivers can also be worthwhile if anglers are patient enough. Set fishing in holes is probably the most feasible way to get fish away from dam areas. With an egg sinker, floating jig head rig, a chub can be fished clear through a bottom depression by lifting the rig every so often, then slowly paying out line as the current carries the bait farther on into the hole.

Around the dams themselves, the washout hole below flood gates is the best location for daylight excursions after winter walleyes. They can be thoroughly covered with either slip sinker rigs, slip bobbers left to drift around, or vertical jigging with a lead head. In all cases, live minnows are the bait of choice. All the angler needs other than that is the stamina to withstand the cold, perhaps a catalytic heater and electric socks, for these winter fish.

Chapter 18

Pike & Musky Schemes

"Mere machines for the assimilation of other organisms", is an apt quote describing the two main members of the pike family, *Esox masquinongy* the Muskellunge and *Esox lucius* the Northern Pike. Both species are likely to make meals of minnows, frogs, leeches, panfish, ducks, muskrat, snakes, carp, walleyes, and bass, along with a host of other creatures, including their own kind. With such reputations, it is little wonder that the wolves of freshwater are favorites of the live bait crowd. Why Not? When you can angle for fish that operate on a principle, "If it fits eat it and if not try it anyway!", one is bound to catch his share.

Distribution of the pike encompasses a greater range than that of the muskellunge due to their ability at readily adapting to varied environments. Fishermen are likely to come across northerns in most all of Canada through New York, south to Pennsylvania then west to Missouri, and finally north to the Dakotas and part of Montana. Further plantings, although far from being entrenched, have spread *lucius* to states like Nevada, Georgia, Arizona, Texas, Washington, Colorado, Arkansas, Tennessee, and a few others.

rt.

Natural musky enclaves cover the Great Lakes Basin states and southern Canada into New York, Pennsylvania, then through the Allegheny Mountains into West Virginia, Tennessee, and Kentucky. Like pike, they too have been stocked in states such as the Dakotas, Nebraska, California, Texas, Georgia, South Carolina, Missouri, and Maryland.

Being close relatives that they are, pike and musky resemble each other dramatically. Besides their reknown face full of teeth, the *Esox* family has good eyesight that can differentiate some twenty or more hues according to laboratory studies. Northern also exhibit a keen sense of smell, which can only make things more prosperous for the live bait angler.

The differences between the species is first of all that of coloration, with pike possessing light spots on a dark background, usually dark greyish or brown to green. Muskies carry the reverse, dark spotted markings on lighter background, and in addition have a barred, plain pale, and striped patterned phase in the family. Nowadays, anglers must also be aware of a hybrid in the group, specifically the Tiger Musky, which is a cross between northerns and 'lunges with the traditional dark on light of the musky only in a tiger striped body pattern. Behavior wise, they are more like the pike half, another benefit to the fishing public.

Other distinctions worth checking on the part of an angler are sensory pores on the bottom of the lower jaw and scales on the cheek and gill covers. Pike average 10 pores, hybrids 10-12, and true musky average 14 with numbers running from 11-18. True Muskellunge also show a lock of scales on both the lower half of gill cover and cheek. Pike, on the other hand, have cheeks that are fully scaled, and scales on the upper half of the gill cover only.

Spring Fishing

If seasons are open, pike and musky chasers can begin their open water angling year as soon as the ice begins to depart, although fish will already be gathered, and in some cases spawning already. Pike begin their egg laying in waters that range from 40-46 degrees, followed by walleyes, perch, and then musky when temps arrive at the 48-56 degree scale. In bodies that contain both species, time difference is mainly the reason for pike gaining the upper hand over their cousins as dominant predators. However, both species will begin movements that provide fishing as soon as water nears forty where the males are concerned.

Location is the key for bait fishermen at this early stage of the game. Fish will be looking for suitable spawning sites, which means shallow, weedy areas with soft sand/muck bottoms and off-colored water. Likely spots will include bayous, bays, weedy flats, and feeder creeks with marshy sections along their sides.

In order to maximize the chances to work on active fish, live baiters should look specifically for spots in these areas that are protected from wind. This will let the sun warm up those fish present as their bodies will absorb heat in the shallow confines of a foot or two of water. It will also behoove anglers not to get rambunctious and head out too early in the day. From high noon on, things will stand a better chance to warm up enough to provide the action they seek.

On larger waters, rather than exploring all over the place, anglers can rely on funnels to provide them with some early fishing also. By funnels, the reference is towards a narrow inlet leading to a bay, patches of advanced weed growth, or the entrance to a shallow feeder stream and the like, anything out of the ordinary that might congregate these early fish in a small area.

For either northerns or musky at this early stage, nothing beats minnows and waterdogs. During this juncture of the seasons that heralds the change from winter to summer, baitfish like chubs, shiners, and suckers make up the contents of most bait buckets, and in the case of northerns, dead bait will take fish also, particularly the larger ones.

In this shallow environment, a pair of polarized sunglasses will help anglers to spot fish, which are then cast to as one option. With the aid of a split shot, the baitfish can be retrieved to a spot in front of the fish where it is left to struggle enticingly as the weight anchors it to the spot.

Though surprising to many, big pike are scavengers to a great degree. They have no qualms about picking up fresh, albeit dead, meal from the bottom, often preferring it in fact since it is far less taxing than chasing live minnows. With their sense of smell, takes little effort, and should anglers make use of oily morsels like cisco, smelt, or alewives, a piece of cake for the fish.

Dead bait fishing is simply set fishing either on the bottom or above it by means of suspending a bait, ideal for the spring cold water situation. It can be practiced from shore, and is primarily done so at its place of origin in Europe. The method is made sucessful primarily by location of the bait more than anything else. Therefore it is important for live baiters to again select those funnels mentioned earlier.

Rigging dead baits is done by several systems, depending on how the angler wishes to deploy his offering. For use under a slip bobber, the Swedish hook is the least complicated way, with only that singular type of hook and accompanying sinker such as a shot, and bobber stop normally used with sliptype floats.

Another setup that can be used from shore or boat is labeled as the "Paternoster Rig". In either means, the rod is anchored in a rod holder with a large enough sinker tied to the base of the line to hold it in place on the bottom. This section of line ends up being a snell of sorts as a swivel is tied in at a length above the weight depending on how far off the bottom the bait is to ride. Finally, a wire snell is added by way of another swivel whose top eye the main line has been slipped through. In effect, the wire snell will be able to slide up and down the main line, and twin treble hooks are added to the wire snell.

The reason for two hooks is to allow for an immediate strike upon attack by a hungry northern. The top treble, like the swivel, is allowed to slide by running the wire through its eye so that it can be adjusted to the size of the baitfish, the primary hook being attached to the lip. The trick to using this rig is keeping the rod tip upright and the line taut.

During the early spring, pike and musky fishermen also have to learn to cope with the problem of unstable weather. Cold fronts will push fish into inactivity and refuge, usually in the center of bays and bayous, off the first breaks in main lake areas, and in the holes of feeder streams, and rivers. Fish can also be counted on to go off feed when the spawning process is in progress, both sexes being aggressive participants as the she fish spread their eggs across an area accompanied by males who fertilize them by releasing milt at the same time. Even after egg laying and the resulting recovery period, fish will remain in the shallows, become active once again until warmer temperatures send them back to the main lake and summer patterns.

Summer Fishing

Summer is without a doubt the toughest time for pike fishermen, not quite as bad for musky fanatics. The reason for this discrepancy in two clearly, closely related fish is more or less temperature preference. In the case of large northerns, they relish cool to cold water. On the better pike lakes, those with a lot of acres and depth to go along with it, the elders often go to depths of 50 feet or more to find the right comfort level. Musky will seek deeper water also, but not to the same extent as pike. If northerns cannot go deep, as in the case of a shallow eutrophic lake, they simply stop feeding altogether while muskies will relate to shallow water objects such as downed timber, stumps, and what have you, but go on feeding. Under all circumstances, everything depends on the actual lake type these fish are confined to and the forage present. Some lakes also have the added aspect of summer stratification to consider. As for river fish, they are another matter entirely.

One of the better options for live baiters working deep water lakes is trolling. With that presentation they can explore various depth levels for suspended fish, structures, and cover lots of territory if need be. Trolling can also help summer anglers determine which type of forage these gamefish are relating to in some instances. As an example, consider the differences that can occur on a lake where both perch and cisco may be used at one time or another. While perch will use drop offs in relation to points and other structure, ciscos are open water forage that suspends frequently. Contacting pike or musky along the drop offs tattletails the use of perch, and subsequently the use of the same forage on other parts of the lake with the same overall characteristics.

Both of these deep water forage types are not little fish food. Perch will usually be in the ten inch plus range and ciscos at least as large, so smart anglers will match their offerings to this range

Figure 41. While small fish will remain fairly shallow, adult pike often seek depths of fifty feet or more to find the right comfort levels.

as well. Anything less for the size of the gamefish is like offering King Kong a batch of grapes.

For fishing near the bottom, live bait snells will take fish, but suspenders are best dealt with through the use of single or tandem spinners worked just fast enough to turn the blades, with a baitfish add on of course. Such a marriage also gives pike and musky hunters an added wrinkle in that they can change blade sizes and colors, which is a definite advantage.

Whereas pike go off feed in many instances during the heat of summer, muskies continue to provide action for trophy hunters. On those lakes likely to stratify, musky make heavy use of weed beds, particularly cabbage on those structures that extend out into the lake furthest such as points and sunken islands where forage is large enough and plentiful enough to suit their needs. On shallow lakes with little or no structure like drop offs, and the like, summer musky like to pick a secluded spot in fairly shallow turf with a stump, downed tree, sunken log or some other object as an ambush point.

As with pike, musky can be had on a big single or tandem spin with a minnow add on. Shallow water fish may also take a swipe at a frog — a good sized one — dropped near one of those objects just mentioned. Working the edges of the weedlines can also be done with a large minnow fished under a slip bobber or off a live bait snell worked just fast enough to cover ground. In the instance of working under the float, instead of hooking the minnow under the dorsal as per the norm, lip hook it instead. This way the minnows can be moved without dragging them unnaturally.

Stinger hooks can be used effectively on both pike and musky. The two most productive hook styles are a treble or a wide gapped (point to shaft width) siwash hook. In either case, the stinger is tied at the base of the steel leader with the main hook strung on the leader by threading through the eye, held in place by a piece of plastic tubing. This way, it can be adjusted to the length of the baitfish; stinger near tail, and in the lip the main hook.

Certainly the most reliable water for both summer musky and pike are rivers, underfished though they may be. The key to the bests waters is pools, those lethargic looking stretches of water

Figure 42. Those lethargic looking stretches of water where current is slowed are strongholds for pike, offering the right conditions for them to function at their best as ambush artists.

where current is slowed due to a widening of the shorelines, and depths that are more uniform. Such strongholds give these top of the line predators plenty of room, food, and the right conditions for them to function at their best as ambush artists.

Pike and musky in moving water tend to be object oriented in relation to their feeding station choices. Large boulders, downed trees, stump fields, depressions in the bottom, mid-river humps, bridge abutments, rip-rap, points and their resulting eddies are just a few examples. Fishing such objects in moving water with live baits calls for presentations that allow the fish an easy target they find hard to resist, and yet let the angler have the best angle for a good hook set at the same time. Two options provide the means to accomplish both criterias; fishing directly downstream so the bait passes directly by the fish or quartering to let the bait swing across in front of the fish.

As usual, minnows get the nod, and for both presentations, a fulcrum jig is one way to cover all bets. With their flat heads and tendency to lift or swim due to counteracting forces of flow and tight retrieved line, live bait anglers will have little trouble working them near suspected pike or musky locations.

Fishing bait under bobbers can also be used effectively, especially where current is minimal or in eddies where flow moves back upstream towards the angler. In-line spinners can be useful for the maneuvers called for in river fishing, and a must when waters are stained or muddied from rains.

One other situation should be noted when it comes to river fishing for toothfish, foremost when it comes to pike, that of spring holes. Spring holes are created by cold water entering the mainstream either from underground or through the influx of feeder streams. No matter how it happens, the big drop in temperature draws big pike who may stack up like cord wood in such locations. Live bait fishermen thoughtful enough to stash a thermometer on board and subsequently find one of these gold mines can expect just about anything they throw in them to be attacked by a refreshed northern.

Fall Fishing

Autumn is boom time for pike and musky hunters with the best days of all coming after the turnover. On the deeper lakes, where pike more than not have been lethargic and out of reach due to summer temperatures, fish will move back to relatively shallow water once again. Both species like to take advantage of prey situations, be the formation of mega schools of perch along steep drop offs next to flats, or ciscos in their fall spawning ritual.

Those blustery days carrying the first real fall storms following the turnover see pike and musky roaming the now dying cabbage beds picking off everything from bass to perch heading for deep water. Depending on weather and location, such happenings can occur from September thru November, but it is a time anglers have to experience to believe.

An in-line spinner like the June Bug is dynamite in such locations, tipped with a shiner or chub, and weighted just enough to allow it to barely touch the remaining weed tops.

Another wrinkle in the autumn pike and musky arsenal is the use of leadheads and salamanders on these same flats. Unlike other species, where the jig should be sparsely dressed due to slow metabolism, a fat jig is better, something along the lines of the living rubber variety, for hungry *Esox* members.

With a strong, long rod in the eight to eight and a half foot range, the lead and lizard are worked through the weed beds with a slow lift and drop to the bottom or pure swimming motion.

As with walleyes, cisco spawning sites are prime fall hot-spots because both pike and musky love these preyfish that are soft finned, rich, and easy to capture. During daylight hours both fish will lay off the area, but muskellunge will also follow this food onto the flats after dark when they actually spawn.

Daylight depths depend on the level at which the ciscos are resting. Pike and musky will usually be slightly below or even with their prey. Bobber fishing large suckers is one way to get them for live bait anglers. Simply drifting the suckers, weighted by split shot is another. More precise depth control can also be had where anglers join a bait walker type sinker with the previously marked monofilament line they select for use with a larger bait. However, the additional weight of these rigs calls for a stinger hook to be employed, usually under the dorsal, for a quick strike before a pike or musky detects this abnormality.

Winter Angling

The mainstay of winter fishing for live baiters is the tip-up, and angling is primarily for northerns as musky do not do a lot of winter feeding, if any. Unlike walleye fishing with these crossed bits of wood or aluminum, baits are often times better dead than alive when it comes to northerns.

Smelt, ciscos, alewives, and whole, dead herring are top choices, especially early and late in the season when big northerns prowl the shallows in water less than ten feet. They have to appear lifelike, though movement is not required. Therefore, anglers must either use a Swedish hook, or rig them otherwise so that they set horizontal in the water. When the Swedish model is employed, anglers must remember to keep line tight after initial hook set due to the very small bend at the barb, and its minimal penetration.

For fishermen who cannot sit still for long, an active approach to keep from dying of boredom is jigging spoons like the Swedish Pimple, Hopkins, and similar types. These are tipped with minnows like chubs, or shiners which can stand the strain of constant movement and subsequent strikes without tearing off the hook prematurely.

Jigging through the ice for pike calls for stout rods, and free-spool reels. It is also a good idea to choose dacron over monofilament. The rigors of battle through an ice hole with its rough edges, the cold temmperatures, and mono's known stretch factor all can contribute to lost fish otherwise.

In lakes where trout, cisco, and other open water forage fish are the major food supply, suspension is a very probable situation for winter pikers. On other waters, the edges of drop offs on points, bars, and sunken islands where perch and other warmer water species spend their winter are spots to look for trophies. In a lot of cases, just watching where groups of ice anglers are fishing for other species can lead pike hunters to the fish during the hard water period.

Chapter 19

Trout Trappings

True trout aficionados are as fanatic about their favorite fish as any bass angler, walleye chaser, or musky man. Here in North America, three members of the trout clan hold the widest span of attention, covering both rivers and streams, lakes as well, and virtually all means of fishing, including live bait angling.

The Fish

From restaurant menus to printed words, the Rainbow Trout probably has the greatest exposure to the public, angler and non-angler alike. *Salmo gairdneri* is likely to be found naturally from Northern Mexico to the Aleutian Islands of Alaska in both lakes and streams, not to mention their sea living cousins.

Rainbows are a favorite of fish and game department stocking programs in both lakes and stream environments. Indeed, in those enclosed bodies of water without inlet or outlet feeders, little if any reproduction occurs, so planting is a must to continue a fishery. By any other name, those rainbows that do migrate up a stream or river to spawn, be they lake or anadromous (sea run), are called steelhead.

Inland rainbows spawn from January through August, depending on location with the she fish digging a bedding site (redd) in either riffle areas or the tail end of a pool where the water shallows up. Several batches of eggs may be deposited in different nest sites until the lady is spent, moving back downstream shortly thereafter. Neither parent stays with the eggs or resulting young who may live an average of 5-7 years, if they survive the inherent calamities of their world.

Brown Trout are the fish with a big reputation in this group, most of which is well deserved. Described quite often with adjectives like wary, cunning, and reclusive among others, they are prized for their reluctance to commit suicide on just any old angler's offering. In mixed populations with brook or rainbows, catch ratios will run 4-5 to 1, lending credence to stories of broken hearted brown chasers.

Salmo trutta is not native to this side of the Atlantic, being introduced to the U.S. in 1883, but is now widely available throughout the continent. Of the trouts, browns are notorious for being nocturnally active, especially the large lake dwellers. Like 'bows, they will migrate up rivers and streams, spawning from October through February. They will however lay eggs in enclosed waters as well when the stream option is unavailable, usually in coarse rock or rubble areas.

Browns are indeed the savior of trouting in many places, filling niches that native fish have long since abandoned, especially brook trout. Many bodies of water have needed only one or two plants to establish a population, due as much to their hardiness as their inclination for survival from the onslaught of angling.

If there is one fish that encompasses the image of trout fishing — a secluded wilderness stream with raucous bubbling water surrounded by only woods and sky — it is the Brook Trout. More than anything else, the decline of such habitat in today's pave it — leave it — build more-mentality has brought on the decline of these wild fish native to the Northeast from Georgia to the Arctic Circle.

All is not lost however, as plantings have been made brookies available to trout anglers in most parts of the country. There are some remote mountain streams and lakes too where wild trout are numerous. In lakes, brook trout will spawn over bark and twigs, as well as other debris in either shallow or deep water if they have no flowing waters available for repopulation rites. Egg laying takes place from September thru December, although brookies are far less prolific than their relatives. A fouteen inch she fish will normally only produce a little over a thousand eggs.

In waters where brook trout must share their living quarters with either browns or rainbows, anglers will most likely find *Salvelinus fontinalis* in the upper reaches of streams near the head waters. Lacking appropriate habitat in the midwestern U.S., the best brook trout fishing is for the most part concentrated in small trickles of streams in those out of the way semi-wild sections of the countryside. Trophy waters today are pretty much limited to large rivers in the wilds of Canada such as God's River and the Broadback in Quebec.

In trout circles, there is always talk of temperature when the fish and angling are being discussed. That is as it should be, since temperature is a critical factor in the location process, particularly in lake fishing. Although temperature preferences are close, they do differ enough so that anglers can use them to separate where they are likely to find fish, as well as their activity possibilities. Brook trout use a zone from 57-61 degrees, while browns seek one between 54-63. However, browns are much more tolerant of warm water and can survive heat up to 84 degrees. Brookies have a lethal high of only 77. Rainbows prefer a range from 56-60 given a choice, and their lethal limit maximums are in the mid 80's.

These days acidity, otherwise known as pH, can also be a problem for live baiters in search of trout waters in general, or specific producing areas on a certain body. In the realm of brook trout, they have a pH range of 4.0-9.8. Browns 4.5-9.8, and rainbows 5.8-9.5, or from acid to highly alkaline water.

Stream Fishing
Stream fishing for trout is the bailiwick of both purist and bait

angler, but day in and day out "meat" under all circumstances will outproduce the other alternatives given proper presentation. Trout ingest a wide variety of morsels, so the live bait angler's options are pretty much wide open. This holds true even more so where specimens are large enough to pretty much eat what they please. The various nymph forms, shrimp, worms, minnows, terrestrials such as crickets and grasshoppers, crayfish, grubs, madtoms, leeches and others are all likely picks. As critical to success as choice and presentation for stream and river fishermen is the tackle they choose where live baiting is concerned.

The spinning reel is perhaps the optimum tool for taking fish from moving water, allowing for casting or flipping baits when needed and the capacity to quickly change spools for different line weights to meet conditions. However, the standard spinning rod may not suit the requirements as well as a converted fly rod for waters that may vary enough to cause anglers to lay on their belly, hide behind a bush, crouch down mid-stream or cast half way across a wide body in order to present their lightweight offering to a wary trout. All in all, the lighter, longer fly rod, with reel taped on, is apt to handle such situations for live baiters where trout are the target.

In-stream trout use a wide scope of refuges to accomplish the duo purpose of hiding and eating to sustain their existence. Fallen logs, undercut banks, weed patches, rock and boulders, sunken brush and other structures are all worthy of exploration by live bait anglers. However, such probing must be done in a completely natural manner, entailing that the bait be moving with current nine times out of ten. In order to do that, casts have to be made upstream or quartering, perhaps just dabbling by using the rod to guide the bait past a productive holding station that is close to the angler's position. In all instances, terminal tackle plays an important role in stream trouting as much as the equipment.

Terminal tackle such as sinkers, hooks, and other bits and pieces need not be terribly numerous for stream trouters. That is fortunate since pack mule rentals are at a premium price these days if you can find one when you need it. A variety of split shot sizes, light wire aberdeen or salmon egg hooks from #10 to #6, and

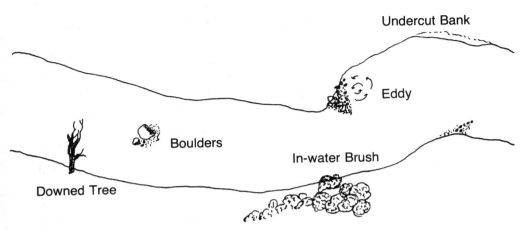

Figure 43. Stream Trout Lairs

perhaps some spinnerblades and their accessories for off color water conditions should stand the fisherman in good stead in all but a few stream situations.

For the stream trout fisherman, where he or she places the hooks in the live baits they select is also an important aspect of their angling. Smaller baits such as nymphs, shrimp, and terrestrials should be hooked once thru the collar behind the head. Smaller worms should also be hooked singularly, thru the breeding ring, and minnows thru the top lip to keep them alive longer and appear natural at the same time. Nightcrawlers can be hooked twice, mid-body so that both ends are left hanging. As for crayfish, they can be nose hooked or strung in the tail, and leeches, once thru the main sucker at the head.

Lake Fishing

Fishing trout in inland lakes is a more complicated aspect if for no other reason than the different locations that fish can be encountered at. They could be a foot below the surface, fifty feet down, suspended in open water or hugging a sunken island, grubbing for nymphs or chasing baitfish.

With all these possibilities, few anglers would argue that trolling is the most logical approach to finding trout in lakes, especially on those bodies unfamiliar to the angler. Additional aids towards narrowing the likely spots would be a temperature probe like the Lowrance Fish-N-Temp, and a pH meter.

Given the fact that trout are attracted by the flash and noise of spinners, blade add-ons to rigs are one of the better selections as part of any trolling setup when searching for lake bound trout. Bait wise, minnows in the shiner family, leeches, and nightcrawlers or leaf worms do the most good for the presentation of moving baits.

The trout family is notorious for slamming into a bait, particularly a moving one, when they are in the confines of a lake. That foregone conclusion means that anglers will have to take heed when it comes to their hook arrangements on the chosen live baits. For minnows, one of the best ways is to employ a long shanked single or double hook style and run it from the anal vent thru the body and out the mouth. Crawlers should be set up on at least a double hook snell so they can be attached once at the head and again beyond the breeding ring. Leeches, being bite sized and tough, are most often gulped all at once so a single hook will be sufficient in their case.

Once fish are located, presentations can change if trout are pretty much stationary, either suspended or working near the bottom. Free floating fish can often be enticed with little more than a slip bobber suspended worm or nymph. Counting down jigs with a nymph, leech, or leaf worm are also worth trying.

Lake fish feeding off a hatch like mayflies will take a wiggler simply presented on a small hook with only enough shot to afford casting weight and left to settle slowly. Bottom huggers will go for tipped leadheads, and nightcrawlers that have been injected with a bubble of air fished off slip sinker rigs as well.

Winter Fishing

Just because it turns cold and freezes is no reason for die hard trouters to give up their sport. Wintertime is one of the better periods for trouting in lake or stream, a natural projection of the sport given the fish's penchant for cold water temperatures. All of the approaches used in other forms of pursuit for species like bluegills, crappies, or pike will catch trout from tip-ups to jigging large or small live bait tipped ice spoons.

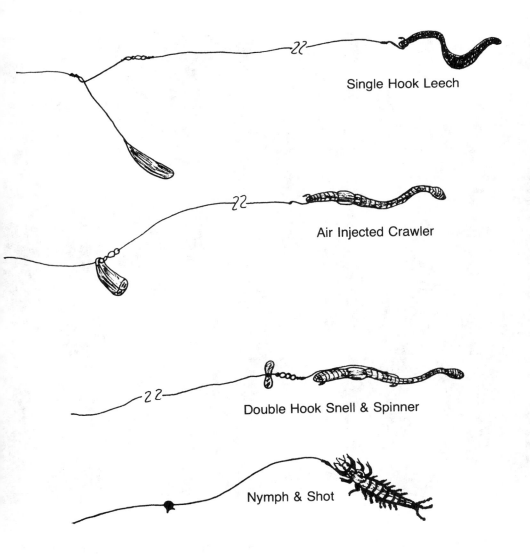

Single Hook Leech

Air Injected Crawler

Double Hook Snell & Spinner

Nymph & Shot

Figure 44. Trout Rigs for Lake Fishing

Figure 45. Bottom hugging trout in lakes will often go for a tipped leadhead.

In the winter, trout do not suspend as much, certainly not as high up as they do in the warmer months. They are also more attracted to water movement like springs and areas close to stream inlets.

Some of the better trout trickers for live baiters to make use of under hardwater are nymphs, grubs, and small minnows no larger than 3-4 inches. While the nymphs and baitfish are best presented with little fanfare other than perhaps a small attractor spoon already mentioned, grubs can be offered on a small wet fly or nymph imitation as well as on the spoons.

With enough water movement and cooperating temperatures, fishing streams and rivers will give up trout too, especially browns and rainbows during the winter. Once again nymphs have the lead position as fish takers, especially when anglers have selected drift fishing as the presentation. When things get downright cold and very slow, set fishing with leaf worms or crawlers worked off a three-way swivel rig is consistent on rivers and streams as well.

Figure 46. Rivers afford catfishermen and women their best chances for success over a prolonged period.

Chapter 20

Catfish Capers

Another likely realm for live baiters to explore is catfishing. Though often thought of as just another bottom feeding scavenger with questionable looks, sporting a love for the smelliest — otherwise raunchy — globs of stinkbait, cats offer plenty of sport. Some members of the order even prefer live — or at least fresh — bait over less fragrant morsels.

Among those catfish capable of supplying the needs of a bait fisherman, namely a fish on the end of his or her line large enough and strong enough to battle well, are the channel, blue, and flatheads. Largest of the trio are the Blues, *Ictalurus furcatus*, which can top out at over 200 pounds. Second in line on the scales are the Flatheads or Yellow Cats, *Pylodictis olivaris*, with an average 4-5 pounds far below their maximum of 100 sixteen ounce pieces. Finally, often nicknamed "Fiddler", Channel Catfish or *Ictalurus punctatus* occasionally reach some fifty pounds.

Both blues and flatheads are primarily fish of big river systems like the Ohio, Mississippi, or Missouri. Channels have been stocked on both coasts, inhabit quite a few lakes, and are at home in both large and small river systems across the land, making them readily available to many anglers. Naturally, this not only makes them more popular, but accessible to fishermen as well. In addition channels actually seek out faster flow, channels if you prefer, and the cleanest of waters with sand/gravel/rock bottoms, even more so than their relatives.

Catfish are not choicy. As far as live bait goes, anglers can count on minnows (alive or just dead), leeches, crayfish, catalpas, leaf and redworms, nymphs, and frogs to catch this fish with feelers. In rivers, where anglers stand their greatest chances of success over a prolonged period, there are a variety of ways to present these fish takers to the catfish clan.

Many successful fishermen prefer to make things as leisurely, or in other words easy, as possible by set fishing from bank or boat. They fish the holes during daylight hours and the flats at night as "Old Whiskers" moves shallower to feed after the sun goes down. This means makes the fish locate the bait on their own with that keen sense of smell they possess, along with the chin and snout whiskers (actually barbels).

Rigs are simple and different from a split shot and hook to slip sinkered snell setups with either egg or worm weights. The bait, minnows-crayfish-worms-catalpas-leeches, is cast out to a probable spot and the rod propped up on a forked stick if on the shore or in a rod holder when boatbound until a cat inhales the offering.

Another means, especially effective on smaller rivers and streams during mid-summer when wading is feasible for live bait anglers involves drift fishing with a slip bobber during daylight hours. This is the time when cats are lounging in holes, washouts, undercut banks, beneath brush piles, and other darkened hideouts. The object is to let the current carry the offering into such likely territory with the depth of the bait set so that it is barely a couple of inches off the bottom in a natural manner.

For some reason, giant grasshoppers are one of the more effective live bait choices for this dog days angling, followed by crawlers, and finally crabs. Minnows and leeches can also prove themselves, but they lend themselves better to a couple of other variations and

and times when catfishing.

During periods of cloudy, drizzly weather, catfish are as active as if it were nighttime, cruising the flats actively seeking any type of meal. A good way for the angler to give them what they seek is with a leech combined with a spin-n-glo.

The terminal outline for such fishing employs a three-way swivel complete with six to eight inch dropper and a dipsey sinker. The snell at the fishing end of the swivel is kept to around a 12 inch length in order to keep the high riding cork spinner close enough to the bottom for the cats to locate it easily. No matter if it is the low hum of the spin-n-glo or the smell of the leech — probably both — cats literally cream the offering when they find it.

Nocturnal angling and minnows go well together, particularly when it comes to elders of the whisker tribe. Live baitfish in the 5-8 inch range such as chubs, shiners, or suckers or dead baits with an aroma like smelt or cisco account for lots of action below dams. Depending on whether the choice is indeed dead or alive, hook setups can vary from under the dorsal or in the lip where minnows are breathing to a double hook quick strike rig if they are dead. In both cases though, most fishermen employ either egg or worm slip sinker to let the fish move off with the bait before a hook set is made.

Sometimes, when cats are a bit off feed — rare though that may be — or conditions such as high water make things a little difficult, a substitution in presentation by way of vertical fishing can be effective, if done from a boat. The procedure is a duplicate of slipping for the likes of walleyes in rivers, with the fishing being done by jig and bait or a bottom probing rig made up of sinker at line end and hook tied about twelve inches above. If the water is discolored, the right way to go is with a juicy bait like a wadded up nightcrawler or catalpa. In clearer H_2O, a jig tipped with piece of worm, crawdad, or hopper will do just fine. Anglers might employ a madtom as well. Cats do not mind eating their own kind either.

Of course, there are the more traditional methods of getting catfish from the water to frying pan, jugging and trot lining being the two most prolific to come to mind. Jugging is best done on stretches of water where currents are not too fast, and depths pretty much uniform and snag free. This way the bait, suspended at a pre-set depth on a gallon jug, will ride downstream smoothly until contact with a hungry fish is made.

Trot lines are a line with a series of baited hooks tied in at intervals along its length, with the snells varying in length depending on where the line is set in order for all to be near or on the bottom. Sometimes they are set from bank to mid-stream, being anchored in place, but most often the set is run along the shorelines which makes them easier to tend after a night's fishing for anglers with no boat. A good way to take numbers of catfish, though fishing with rod and reel is more fun and more sporting for both angler and fish. As for baits, anglers make use of virtually all those mentioned, often mixing them to see which is producing the best for an extended trip.

Chapter 21

Proper Catch And Release

With all the pressures on this modern day sphere in space, fish can use all the help they can get from anglers. On top of development, water traffic, pollution, disease, habitat loss, the strictly meat fisherman and the ever present poacher, along with improper release by otherwise conscientious anglers account for untold thousands of fish deaths. Live baiters should be aware that they must take even more care than other fishermen, given the likelihood of deeper hook intake and its related consequences with their completely edible offerings.

First off, anglers should be cognizant of what goes on when their quarry is hooked, fought, and subsequently landed. Stress factors begin immediately with the lifting of a rod.

One of the primary causes of fish death, even after release, is termed lactic acidosis, or a build up of lactic acid in the muscle tissue and blood stream. The result is an increasing need for oxygen, which when lacking enough causes improper brain function. In other words, shock that harms other vital organs. We humans suffer the same malady to some degree when exercising strenuously, hence sore muscles. The remedy for the fish practiced by the angler is not to overplay that pike, musky, or bass. Get them in the boat, better yet next to it, as quickly as possible.

Landing, then handling a fish is the next problem anglers have to concern themselves with in relation to release. Some fish just by their physical makeup are easier to get unhooked and back into the water than others.

Most fish naturally carry a mucous coating over their skin besides scales. Its purpose is to protect them from infection, parasites, and as an aid in movement. Mishandling that removes this protection, although maybe not apparent at that moment, can cause problems to the fish later.

There is also the aspect of inner organ damage when a fish is out of the water due to the sagging of vital body parts no longer supported by water pressure. Therefore, if a fish must be lifted from its environment, they should never be jerked around or banged against anything.

Ideally, the fish that is to be released should simply be shook off the hook boatside. Barely lip-hooked, this is a breeze, but also a rarity, especially where live bait is concerned. Fish like bass and crappie can be easily handled by gripping the lower lip firmly. Toothy species are a different ball-game. Pike and musky have a muscle at the base of the gill plate where gripping is feasible, but care must be taken so that fingers do not slip into the gills. Walleyes and sauger can be handled by grasping on top of the gill plates rather than at the base where razor sharp edges can cut fingers to shreds.

Species like bluegills do not possess sharp gill plates nor teeth, but they do have a small mouth which presents unique difficulties since these panfish almost always need a bit of handling in order to effect release. For smaller fish, they can be held by one hand with a thumb atop the back and the other four fingers under the belly. Hands should be wet to help hold down mucous removal. Larger fish too wide for holding unless one has hands like the blue ox's owner can be lip gripped with a pair of needle nosed pliers or a hemostat surgical tool. Both tools should have their arms covered by plastic tubing to help ward off injury to the lip and jaw though.

There are other tools that make release a much easier and effective chore for careful anglers. They can also be most helpful when fishermen have the misfortune to impale themselves or their clothing, boat seat, hat and other hook magnets.

One of those angler helpers are called grippers, a spring loaded tool that enables a fish to be held behind the head area across the body. They are primarily for use in handling species like musky, pike, and larger than average catfish. Then there are the various "hook out" tools with a toothed nose whose lower jaw is hinged to afford movement, coupled with hinged handles also. There metal thingamabobs all have long necks for reaching back into the gullet area, and are extremely useful.

Plastic has invaded the realm of release too with what are labeled "hook disgorgers". Most are about 6-8 inches long with a groove cut into the petroleum product for the line to slip into. When the tip of the tool is tight to the hook penetration point, the procedure is to push, and in some cases twist at the same time, to pop the hook out.

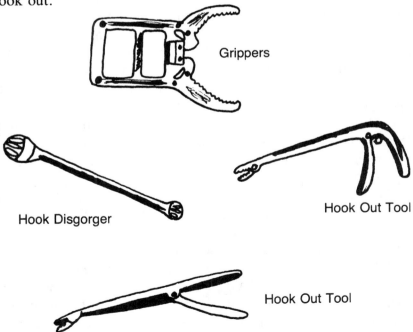

Figure 47. Tools for Effective Release

Where a fish is hooked is paramount in importance to the chances for survival or disability and death. Bleeding does not always mean a fish is beyond help, as is often thought, but on the other hand, a non-bleeder may not live either. Areas of the mouth, gills and throat that afford excellent chances for continued living when invaded by an angler's steel are the lip, frontal roof of the mouth, and gills if not bleeding. Locations with reasonable results if care is taken are the rear of the mouth and tongue, both front and rear. Spots that often give little hope for fish, especially if there is bleeding, are the gullet (esophagus), gills, and deep in the throat or gut. In all cases, if a hook can be remomved without cutting it or the line, by all means do so. Studies have shown that hooks left in to dissolve by rusting are more often than not fatal to the fish.

There are other factors and things anglers can do to help those finny denizens who cooperate by trying to eat their offering. Fishing in the cool or cold water periods of spring, fall, and winter is an aid in itself. Slower metabolic rates requiring less oxygen consumption lowers stress. Warmer waters have less capacity for carrying oxygen, thus increasing the need for fish to acquire it even without the exertion of a battle with anglers. For fish, O_2 consumption is doubled or tripled by every twenty degree rise in water temperature.

Other commercial aids available to fishermen who wish to acquire them can help stave off infections and assist in healing some damaged areas, particularly for fish held in live wells prior to return to their world. One of these is tetracycline hydrochloride, along with acriflavine and furacin, all of which can be had from a pet store or vet supply house.

One commercial product available in many tackle shops these days is Jungle Laboratories, "Catch and Release". This mixture is designed to be added to live wells, and is a tranquilizer, lactic acid neutralizer, slime or mucous production stimulant, and restorer of blood pressure. Coupled with careful handling and unhooking procedures, all of these added aids are a boon to the catch and release principle. For the future of angling, it all adds up to tomorrow's pleasure versus an alternative like taking up golf or tennis. Both are pleasureable pastimes, but then again golf and tennis balls are not known for leaps silhouetted by a sunrise or being in the least bit edible no matter who is doing the cooking.

INDEX

tannic acid, 11
temperature, nightcrawlers, 7-8
thermocline, 117
Tiger Musky, 165
Tiger Salamander, 24
tissue paper, 4
tools, worm harvesting, 3, 15
topographic map, 26
treble hook, 84
Tubifex, tubifex, 14
tuna and albacore hook, 84

ultraviolet rays, effects, 8
U.S. Geological Survey, 26

Walleye, 151-163
   range, 153
   spawn, 154
wasp larvae, 63
Wax Moth, 72
Wax Worm- See Beemoth
weedless hook, 84
Wheeler and McGregor, reels, 94
White Crappie, 123
White Sucker, 48
Wiggler- See Mayfly
wire trap, baitfish, 49, 51
worm development, 13
worm harvesting, 4-6, 11-12
worm sinker, 98, 100

Yellow Bullhead, 71
Yellow Catfish- See Flathead Catfish
Yellow Perch, 115-121
   range, 115
   spawn, 115-116

zooplankton, 114